As in the

Day

of

Midian

Dr. Susan Marie Pender

Published by Lovett Press International
ISBN: 978-1-937045-54-8
Printed in the United States of America

Scripture quotations NIV are from the Holy Bible Thompson Chain-
Reference Bible New International Version, copyright © 1990 by The
B.B. Kirkbride Bible Company, Inc. Indianapolis, Indiana.

Scripture quotations TPT are from The Passion Translation®, copyright
© 2017, 2018 by Passion & Fire Ministries, Inc. Used by permission.
All rights reserved. ThePassionTranslation.com.

Scripture quotations MSG are from THE MESSAGE, copyright ©
1993, 2002, 2018 by Eugene H. Peterson. Used by permission of
NavPress. All rights reserved. Represented by Tyndale House
Publishers, Inc.

Scripture quotations KJV are from the Authorized King James Version,
Zondervan Publishing House, Grand Rapids, Michigan copyright ©
1964, 1965, 1966 by Royal Publishers, Inc. Nashville, Tennessee

Scripture quotations NKJV are from the NKJV Spirit-Filled Life Bible
Third Edition copyright 2018 by Thomas Nelson, Published in Nashville,
Tennessee by Thomas Nelson, a registered trademark of HarperCollins
Christian Publishing, Inc.

Scripture quotations AMP are from the Amplified Bible, copyright ©
2015 by The Lockman Foundation La Habra, CA 90631.
Scripture quotations NLT are from the New Living Translation,
copyright © 2004 Tyndale House Publishers, Wheaton, Ill

For speaking engagements or questions
Contact Susan Marie Pender
Susanmariepender@gmail.com
www.lilyofthevalleyhealing.com

Dedication

I dedicate this work to all the prayer warriors, intercessors, pioneers, and forerunners in the Lord who have labored in the region of the Northern Red River Valley Territory. You have plowed in this region through consistent prayer and spiritual warfare mostly in the secret places of your lives. This has been a labor of love for God and for the people. May we all fulfill our call and purpose out of love for the Lord, and for our children, and our children's children, and our children's children's, children. May each generation experience the goodness of God and experience an encounter with Him that they may know Him.

For you have broken the yoke of his burden, And the staff of his shoulder, The rod of his oppressor, as in the day of Midian.

Isaiah 9:4, NKJV

Acknowledgments

Thank you, Ann Lovett Baird for your skills and creative abilities in editing, formatting, and designing of covers to enable the publishing of books. I honor your gifting and abilities. You are a student of the Word and find joy in learning and discovering new revelation in your walk with the Lord. Thank you for using your gifting to help me and others. I'm grateful for you.

Table of Contents

Introduction

God speaks to everyone whether they know Him or not, whether they have a relationship with Him or not. God speaks through dreams, an audible voice, an inner witness, which is the still small voice inside, through other people, through nature, and even through animals. Most of the time when God speaks, people tend to think they are hearing their own thoughts or their own voice inside and do not recognize that God is talking to them.

When we read in the Bible that God spoke to people audibly, or through a burning bush, the wind, a donkey, in a dream, or in a soft whisper, then we can begin to recognize God's voice in our own lives.

On December 10, 2010, I got out of bed at 3:00 am and went to look out my kitchen window. It was winter in northern Minnesota, and everything was frozen, covered with a thick blanket of beautiful white snow. The moonlight glistened on top of the snow-covered ground revealing an absolute peaceful countryside view. While standing alone in my home at my window looking at this picturesque scene, I heard the Lord say in a sweet gentle calm voice, "There is something big coming."

No fear or dread reflected in His voice. There was absolutely no alarm about what He spoke to me. He was just letting me know, that there was something big coming and it would be the opposite of the beautiful peaceful scene that I was looking at.

A few days after this, I woke up in the morning knowing I had seen God in what must have been a dream. I saw Him step down from Heaven to Earth to walk through our city and rural area. I saw Him looking into houses and businesses to observe how the people were living. I saw Him walk through the streets and down the country roads looking into every home. He was taking a close look into our private lives. I could tell He had a father's heart for the people but was saddened by what He saw.

When God told me "Something big is coming," I had a sense that He wanted to help us and intervene for us because what was coming would require His help and all of Heaven's assistance. But we would need to turn our hearts toward Him to receive this divine help. We would need to repent and turn away from our selfish ways. If we remained stubborn and rebellious, not turning our hearts to His fatherly kindness and goodness, then it would not be good for us at the time we needed His intervention. If God had really come down to take a close-up look at our lives, like I had seen, I knew it was for a reason.

On March 18, 2011, I was attending a conference at Mike Bickel's church in Kansas City. During one of the sessions at this conference, there was a teaching on the gift of prophecy and how it is for exhortation, edification, and comfort. The gifts of the Holy Spirit mentioned in 1 Corinthians 12, are not to bless the holder of the gift, but to bless other people and to help equip others to become mature saints in their faith in Christ. It was during this session that I received a prophetic word from the minister who was instructing us.

"You have been pregnant a long time. It is time to go to the hospital and have this baby. There are Herods out there who would want to come along and rob from you. Partake in the feast of Esther if you know what that is."

March 18, 2011

Given to Susan Pender by Frank Bray

As in the Days of Midian

I had heard of the feast of Esther, called Purim, but had never participated in it personally or corporately. In this historical event, Esther was chosen to be the Queen by King Ahasuerus. Esther's parents died when she was a young child so Mordecai, her older cousin, took her in, to care for her and raise her. Through a long purification process, King Ahasuerus chose Esther to be his Queen. Mordecai sat at the king's gate so that he could hear word of how his beloved adopted daughter Esther was doing. While sitting at the gate one day, Mordecai heard two of the king's eunuchs conspiring to kill the king. Mordecai disclosed this to Esther who shared it with the king.

Shortly after this, King Ahasuerus promoted Haman, a court official to King Ahasuerus, giving him authority over all the officials who were with him. The king also ordered all the servants who served at the gates to bow down and pay homage to Haman. Now, Mordecai was also sitting at the gate near the king's palace, but Mordecai refused to bow down to Haman as he came by. This was evident to Haman and infuriated him so much that he devised a plan to destroy Mordecai and all the people of his nationality, the Jewish people. This would include Queen Esther.

Haman deceived King Ahasuerus by telling him there was a people group in his kingdom that did not acknowledge the king's laws and sought permission to have them all destroyed. The king agreed with Haman by signing Haman's evil decree with his signet ring of authority. This gave Haman the right to carry out his evil plot to kill Mordecai and all the Jewish people in King Ahasuerus' kingdom. Word was sent to all the Jewish people along with the day that this would be carried out upon them. Meanwhile, Haman constructed a gallows at his home so he could personally witness Mordecai's hanging because he had refused to bow down to him.

Mordecai heard about this evil plan while he was sitting at the gate. He put on sackcloth and fasted and cried out to the Lord for help. Mordecai sent word to Esther of this evil plan Haman devised. He requested Esther to go before King Ahasuerus to ask him not to allow this decimation to occur. Esther sent a reply to Mordecai explaining that no person including her could go before the king for any reason unless they are summoned. If they did go before the king without being called for, the king had the right to put them to death for dishonoring him. King

As in the Days of Midian

Ahasuerus had already put Queen Vashti to dea for disobeying him. Esther feared for her life if she did nothing to save the Jewish people, and she feared for her life if she did go before the king for help.

Mordecai sent word back to Esther saying, that if she did not go to the king for help now when she had the chance, that she would perish along with all her people. He continued to explain to Esther that going before the king for help was their only chance for survival at this time. Mordecai explained to Esther that perhaps she had favor to receive this position of Queen just for the purpose of saving her people, and if she would choose to remain silent at this time, their liberation would eventually arise from another place.

Esther chose to fast for three days from consuming any food and from drinking any water. She sent word to Mordecai to request all the Jewish people to do the same fast while they seek God for a plan of intervention to save them from annihilation. After the three days ended, Esther went before King Ahasuerus to invite him and evil Haman to dine with her. She understood that the king could order her to be put to death, but Esther was willing to risk that outcome. She had to somehow disclose to the king that

Haman was an evil man who had planned to annihilate her and all the Jewish people. Esther had to be wise, relying on God's intervention in revealing all of this. During the first dinner celebration, Esther did not feel led to disclose Haman's evil plan to the king, so she requested the king and Haman dine with her again the next evening.

That night King Ahasuerus could not sleep and requested to see the books of memorial deeds so he could read through them. It was revealed in those books that Mordecai was the man that saved his life when he exposed the two eunuch's plan to kill him. The next day King Ahasuerus rewarded Mordecai which again infuriated Haman because Haman was forced to honor Mordecai. That evening Haman attended the planned banquet with Esther and King Ahasuerus. Esther disclosed to the king that she was Jewish, and Haman had order her to be killed along with all of her nationality. For this, King Ahasuerus ordered that Haman be hanged on the gallows that had been prepared for Mordecai. Further, the king gave all of Haman's property and possessions to Esther and gave his signet ring of authority to Mordecai. Esther then wrote decrees to reverse the evil decrees that Haman had written against them allowing the Jewish people to be prepared to avenge their enemies. Therefore, Esther and her nation were not destroyed, but saved by fasting and intercession and the unfolding of God's divine plan of intervention.

This story of Esther represents the role intercessors and prayer warriors play in seeking God for answers and intervention from their enemies. The Bible is full of stories that tell of God's goodness in fighting for people and redeeming lives because someone on earth sought God's help. This causes the people to see the reality of God's fatherly love for them which turns their hearts toward Him and away from sin and evil.

Having heard God say, "something big is coming," and then seeing God in a dream looking into our homes, I considered the prophetic word I received in March of 2014 encouraging me to celebrate Purim. I fasted for three days like Esther did, then prepared a meal for the king (God Almighty) and brought my requests before Him.

In our personal walk with the Lord, many times we appear strange when we apply stories like this to our own lives. God does speak to us through scripture and gives us historical stories like this for our personal admonition and direction. Walking out our lives as believers in Jesus

Christ, through the ups and downs, through tests and trials, and through discovering God by reading the Bible and applying it to our everyday lives, is anything but mundane. I received this prophetic word instructing me to celebrate Purim and wanted to obey it. This story of Esther demonstrates the reality of applying Ezekiel's words to our lives.

I looked for someone among them who would build up the wall and stand before me in the gap on behalf of the land so I would not have to destroy it, but I found no one.
Ezekiel 22:30, NIV

Esther asked for the lives of her people. So, would I, but I wasn't sure who my people were. I knew I would surely ask for my children and my family to be forgiven of their sins and to receive God's mercy and to be saved. I planned to include my community, the people who I grew up with and had known all my life. Then I thought, I should ask for the people in the territory of the Northern Red River Valley to receive God's mercy and to be saved by God's great outstretched arms of grace because this was the territory where God had come down to look at the people's lives.

Ask of Me, and I will give You The nations for Your inherit
ance, And the ends of the earth for Your possession.
Psalm 2:8, NKJV

Later that year I retired and relocated to Florida to attend a ministry college for four years. I discovered this ministry college was the hospital the Lord was speaking to me about in that prophetic word. I was pregnant in a spiritual sense with promises, prophetic words, and with the seed of God's written word that had been planted in the soil of my heart over many years. Just as in the natural, giving birth to a baby takes time and requires some assistance. Giving birth in the spiritual realm takes time and requires some assistance also.

A human baby needs to grow for nine months within a mother's womb, then the baby might take many hours and even require surgical intervention for the baby to be born. Many times a baby doesn't survive the full nine months or the birth process. All of this is true in the spiritual realm too. It takes time for spiritual things to develop in us before we come to the place of giving birth to them and seeing them manifest in the natural. People may receive a word from the Lord or a promise, or a prophetic word, but never see it come to pass. They were impregnated, so to speak with a word, but they did not come to the place of birth for various reasons including lack of direction, distractions, cares of the world, not enough strength to bring it forth, or just a lack of knowing they had a seed planted in them that needed to be cared for.

During these four years at the ministry college, I received a lot of teaching, training, mentoring, love, kindness, godly relationship, hugs, inspired prophetic words, and deliverance that repaired the broken places of my heart. This spiritual hospital-like environment enabled me to write my testimonies on paper and to process them mentally and emotionally thus giving birth to books. As we say *yes* to the Lord and walk with Him, good things happen. As I wrote and processed difficult parts of my life, it brought healing to the wounded areas of my soul, thus giving birth.

We can give birth to many different things such as writing a book or song, starting a business, having a creative idea for an invention, or how to do something more economically. We could give birth to answers to long-standing questions or develop a new medical procedure. There is no end to what God can birth through us as we say *yes* to Him.

After finishing these four years of college, I was not sure what my next step was. I could stay in Florida in this wonderful community of believers and possibly travel and minister with some of them. I had not even considered returning to the place where I had come from. God told me through several prophetic words that He wanted me to slow down and spend more time with Him. Sometimes, in order to hear God speak to us, we have to slow our lives down and sit quietly with Him. I knew He wanted to help me with my next step.

The best step anyone can take in their life, is one that they hear from God and act on.

Standing in the Gap for a Territory

Into my fifth year in Florida, late one January night of 2019, I was asking the Lord about my next steps when I heard the Lord say, "Remember that territory you asked me for?"

Immediately I knew what He was talking about. In the busyness of walking out my own restoration, taking college courses, writing, and working as a nurse during the night, I had forgotten that I had asked God for a certain territory. Now in my fifth year of being mentored, trained, and restored, the Lord reminded me of a request I brought before Him during that Purim celebration in 2014. I wrote down what I wanted for myself, my children, my family, my community, and the territory that I lived in. My request was that we not be annihilated but preserved. Having seen God walk through our streets to observe how we were living, gave me a concern for the people. There was a time coming that we would need God's intervention, so I requested of the king (God Almighty) that the people in this territory would be saved and preserved.

As in the Days of Midian

As God reminded me of my request to intervene for us in this territory, I realized He was telling me to go back. It was a deep realization that God does hear our prayers and has intentions to grant our requests, just like He did for Esther! God really does have plans to save, redeem, and to restore us and to supernaturally protect and preserve us.

During the next few months, God prepared my heart by continually confirming to me to return home. This caused me to question the boundaries of this Northern Red River Valley Territory. God sets the boundaries of our lands and waterways, and He has reasons for doing it the way He does. So, I felt it was important for me to research these boundaries. It is the same as asking God for a nation; we should know where that nation is geographically located.

To find out the boundaries of that region, I contacted the Hjemkomst Historical Center in Moorhead, Minnesota to inquire what they had to say about the boundaries of the Red River Valley territory. Their reply was that there are no set boundaries for the Red River Valley territory because people look at it in several different ways. These are the different perspectives of those views. These perspectives show the difference between the valley and that valley's territory, which includes the area affected by the drainage of its waters.

1. First, it is defined by the individual counties on each side of the Red River.

2. Second, it is defined by the railroad because grants were received to market the name of the Red River Valley.

3. Third, it is defined by the original Lake Agassiz glacial basin, which stretches from South Dakota to the Hudson Bay, Canada.

4. Lastly, it is defined by the Lake Agassiz glacial basin drainage, which covers a larger region than just the original glacial basin, from South Dakota to Hudson Bay in Canada and from Montana through North Dakota to Minnesota.

This is a picture of the Agassiz glacial basin. The drainage extends beyond the highlighted basin.

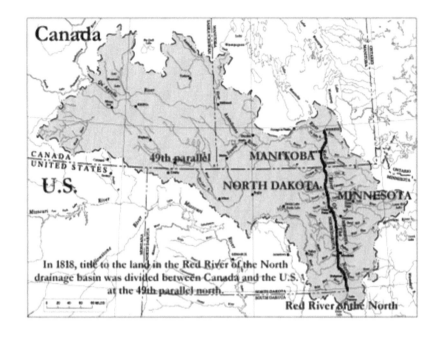

Canada

CANADA
UNITED STATES

U.S.

49th parallel

MANITOBA

NORTH DAKOTA

MINNESOTA

In 1818, title to the land in the Red River of the North drainage basin was divided between Canada and the U.S. at the 49th parallel north.

Red River of the North

Spiritual Mapping/Surveying a Region

I sat under Martha Lucia, an intercessor and watchman associated with Christian International ministries, and her teachings. From my connection with her and studying her books, I gleaned the concept of spiritual mapping or in other words surveying a city or region. This is the same concept that Nehemiah used in rebuilding the walls and gates of Jerusalem. Spiritual mapping or surveying a city or region is a concept of identifying many things, such as landmarks, roads, waterways, the culture of the people, and what they worship or celebrate. This is for the purpose of repenting for the people in that city or region and praying for them to prosper and be blessed of the Lord.

Surveying is done in the natural and can also be done in the spiritual realm. Survey means to examine and record the dimension of a particular area of the earth's surface. Also noted on a survey are the manmade structures, such as a road or building. Once these assessments are taken, they can be used to reveal features of an area of land, in order to create a map, plan, or description. This same concept was used by Nehemiah as he assessed the boundaries of Jerusalem so he could begin rebuilding, repairing, and restoring that city.

In looking at the boundaries of the Northern Red River Valley territory, an interstate highway runs all through this region from mid-Montana all through North Dakota, through Minnesota and beyond. I do not normally look up numbers when seeking insights from the Lord, but this highway stood out to me. Because this interstate was the number 94, I searched through all the books of the Bible for any combination of 94. Only Isaiah 9:4 was a relevant scripture for what God might be speaking into this region of what His plans and intents are for the people.

As in the Days of Midian

For as in the day of Midian's defeat, you have shattered the yoke that burdens them, the bar across their shoulders, the rod of their oppressor.

Isaiah 9:4, NIV

The abuse of oppressors and cruelty of tyrants – all their whips and cudgels and curses - Is gone, done away with, a deliverance as surprising and sudden as Gideon's old victory over Midian.

Isaiah 9:4, MSG

God likes it when we search out the scriptures to gain an understanding of what He is speaking to us. This is how we have relationships with Him. It is part of our journey of faith and the history that we gain in our relationship of walking with Him. He tells us enough to place an yearning inside of us to search out a matter. Then it is up to us whether we take those steps or not.

It is the glory of God to conceal a matter; to search out a matter is the glory of kings.
Proverbs 25:2, NIV

We must study, pray and receive revelation to know what God is speaking. I would need to research who the Midianites were, what yokes burdened the people, what the bars across their shoulders that weighed them down were, in order to hear and understand what God's strategy was to deliver us.

Since arriving at Christian International ministries in 2014, I attended their morning prayer whenever I could. It was during this morning prayer time in January 2019, that the Lord impressed upon me that Bishop Hamon should conduct a City Tour in this region, in Fargo, North Dakota. Bishop Hamon had been conducting City Tours for several years throughout the United States for the purpose of creating an open Heaven so angels would come down to assist believers who were willing to be warriors. The tours

19

were also meant to establish an apostolic fort or apostolic center where warrior angels were dispatched under the Lord's direction to war on behalf of the people. The purpose for these City Tours was also to expose the strongman in that territory and give the people a strategy to overtake that strongman by teaching the people how to conduct warfare intercession and exhorting them to become warriors.[1]

This book reveals the outcome of that City Tour, exposes the strongman network in that region, and gives God's strategy for overcoming in that region; thus, it will be "As in the day of Midian."

City Tour: Expose the Strongman, Become a Warrior

To better understand the purpose of these City Tours, let's look at church history to see how we got to this place in time and where the church is going. God is building His church and the gates of hell will not prevail against it.

And I also say to you that you are Peter, and on this rock, I will build My church, and the gates of Hades shall not prevail against it.
Matthew 16:18, NKJV

Adam and Eve were the first people created by God to live in the earth. They walked and talked with God every day in the Garden of Eden. Satan was also in the Garden of Eden. He was previously known by the name Lucifer. Lucifer was created by God to be the worship leader in Heaven, but when he became so prideful and wanted to be exalted above God, God had Lucifer stripped of his beauty and gifting and removed him from the third heavenly realm casting him down to Earth. When Adam and Eve sinned by

21

disobeying God, they could no longer carry God's glory upon them. They forfeited their authority to govern the earth to the one who had deceived them, satan. Now, satan gained an authority and power and set up his evil kingdom of fallen angels in the earth realm.

When Jesus Christ came into the earth 4,000 years later, He paid for the sins of mankind dying on the cross shedding His own blood. Jesus then went to hell and took back the keys of authority from satan and rose out of hell to sit at the right hand of God in heaven to rule and reign forever.

When we receive Jesus Christ as our savior, we are saying that we believe in all that Jesus did and that our sins can be washed away and that now we are as much of a new creation as Adam and Eve were when they walked and talked with God in the Garden of Eden. When God cleansed and saved us, all of our past sins were removed from us, and we were given the right to become the children of God and heirs of His power and authority. Now, Jesus rules and reigns in the earth through born again believers. When Jesus went to heaven the Holy Spirit was released to come to earth and be with us to comfort, counsel, guide, and assist us. Supernatural gifts were released to us so we could heal the sick, raise the dead, and cast out demonic spirits. The church, or the Ekkelsia has a corporate anointing to remove principalities and powers from their region. Believers in Jesus Christ are the hands and feet of Jesus. They are the body of Christ in the earth.

When Jesus was born into the earth and then died paying the price of sin and death, the Holy Spirit was then able to come into the earth realm to live in people's hearts. Before this time, there were no born-again people. This coming of the Holy Spirit marked the First Reformation because it signified the birth of the Ekkelsia. When the Holy Spirit came on Pentecost into the Upper Room, that was the birth of the Church. That was the beginning of the Church functioning in the earth as a governing body. The Church is the body of Christ, or the bride of Christ. These believers preached and demonstrated the kingdom of God just like Jesus had taught them to do. They were persecuted and martyred by the religious people who still operated and lived by the law of Moses.

When Jesus came and died for our sins, this began the New Covenant of grace and did away with the law. The law of Moses was given to the people so they knew how to

23

live according to God's ways. When Jesus came signifying the New Covenant of grace, we were now commanded to love one another as Christ loved us and in so doing, we will be keeping the law of Moses. But the Pharisees and Sadducees who were the religious teachers in that day continued to uphold their religious ways and rituals that had been done in the past. Eventually, they demanded for Jesus to be put to death because he claimed to be the son of God and they thought it was blasphemy. They didn't want Jesus healing the sick and giving their hearts to him because it took away from the religious influence and power that the Pharisees and Sadducees had over the people.

The First Reformation lasted 500 years, then the Dark Ages came and there were no more writings by the church. The church had gone into apostasy because most of them were killed and the few remaining were forced to abandon the teachings of Jesus Christ. The Pharisees and Sadducees martyred millions of Christ's followers. The Dark Ages lasted until 1500 AD.

The Second Reformation began when Martin Luther joined the monastery and read the Bible only to discover he was saved by grace through faith. He got the revelation that, "The just shall live by faith and by grace are you saved through faith." They called him a heretic and cast him out of the church. This was the beginning of the Protestant movement that manifested through three churches; the Lutheran church in Germany, the Presbyterian church which started in Scotland, and the Episcopalian church which began in England. These three churches were called to maintain the truth of salvation that God restored. The Catholics maintained the Apostles Creed all through the Dark Ages, but they martyred millions of Protestants because they could not receive the new revelation God wanted to give to his church. God had to release the revelation of the truth of the gospel to the church to build it again, because it was almost completely destroyed during the Dark Ages.

In the 1600's, people got the revelation that baptism should be by immersion and not just by sprinkling. So, the Baptist began immersion. This was when the Catholics and Protestants martyred millions of the Baptist. The Baptist maintained these doctrines that were established in 1600.

Then in the 1700's, God moved again and John Wesley got the revelation that we could be holy. This began the Methodist church, Church of God, and Holiness churches. The truths being added to the church were being maintained by new denominations, but others moved on as new revelation was revealed. The maintaining churches of each new revelation, persecuted the pioneering churches who received the next revelation God was giving to them.

In 1800's, A.B. Simpson was an Episcopalian preacher in New York who was told by his doctors that he had only three months to live. Reading his bible, he got the revelation that healing was in the atonement of Christ and began preaching divine healing. Prior to that healing had not been a doctrine that was preached. Someone has to get the revelation and then someone has to pioneer it. Martin Luther pioneered it. John Wesley pioneered it. The Baptist pioneered it and now A.B. Simpson was pioneering it.

In the 1900's, there was a hunger for God by the holiness people. They prayed for revival and received the Holy Spirit and began speaking in tongues. Someone got the revelation and pioneered it. Receiving new revelation, often means that they will have to leave their present church in order to practice their new revelation.

It was in the 1950's the evangelist was restored. In the 1960's the pastor was restored. Then in the 1970's the

26

teacher was restored. In the 1980's the prophet was restored and in the 1990's the apostle was restored. These are known as the five-fold ministries. They are five roles that God has called Christians to fill for the purpose of equipping the body of Christ to maturity. This was the first time in the history of the church since the Early Church that all five-fold ministries had been restored.

And he Himself gave some to be apostles, some prophets, some evangelists, and some pastors and teachers, for the equipping of the saints for the work of ministry, for the edifying of the body of Christ.
Ephesians 4:11-12, NKJV

In 2000, the Saints Movement began which demonstrated the gifts of the Holy Spirit.

In 2008, it is believed by leaders in the Body of Christ that was when the Third Reformation began, although it was not activated until 2016.

Now, it is believed by most bible scholars that in 2016 the Army of the Lord Movement began. Victory must be won in prayer in the spirit realm before it can be won in the natural realm. This is the time for spiritual warriors to take their positions and function in their God-given sphere

27

and purpose. There have always been spiritual warriors or Christians who pray knowing they have an enemy to overcome. The Old Testament and New Testament give many examples for us to gain knowledge and wisdom of who our enemies are. Our enemies are spiritual beings and not the flesh of man. Spiritual demonic beings' function through real people, but when believers by faith pray and make decrees, they overcome spiritual enemies. This is manifesting the Kingdom of God on earth like Jesus did.

This brings us current in the history of the church and gives an understanding of the purpose in identifying and demolishing strongholds. The purpose of Christian International conducting City Tours across the United States included the following.

- To make an open Heaven for angels to come down to assist believers who were willing to be warriors.
- To establish an apostolic fort or center where warrior angels are dispatched under the Lord's direction to war on behalf of believers.
- To expose the strongman in a territory.
- To give the people a strategy to overtake the strongman.
- To teach the people how to do proper warfare intercession for their territory.
- To exhort the people to become warriors.

City Tour: Expose the Strongman, Become a Warrior

In August of 2019 Bishop Hamon, along with a team from Christian International, came to Fargo, North Dakota to share and carry out these purposes. By revelation, this team agreed there were three principalities that make up the strongman over the Northern Red River Valley territory. These included: Freemasonry, Religion, and Witchcraft.[2]

For we do not wrestle against flesh and blood, but against principalities, against powers, against the rulers of the darkness of this age, against spiritual hosts of wickedness in the heavenly places.
Ephesians 6:12, NKJV

There are several things that this City Tour team teaches and assists the people in doing so they can wage an effective warfare to dismantle the strongholds over a territory. They create an open Heaven and establish an Apostolic Center (or fort) for angels to be dispatched under the Holy Spirit's direction by leading the people through prophetic acts and the power of the shout! They lead and demonstrate prophetic warfare intercession as musicians play music, the people war in tongues, and demonstrate prophetic acts. They exhort the people to continue with daily prayer and warfare intercession.

An open heaven is characterized by the manifestation of God's glory and power. This can be seen by healings and miracles taking place. These are supernatural encounters with the holiness of God. Open heavens are created when an individual or group of people worship God in the Spirit and in truth.

As an example of a scriptural warrior, Bishop Hamon brought the message of Gideon and the Midianites. This was a confirmation of the scripture Isaiah 9:4. This scripture and teaching would hold the strategy God was releasing to believers in that territory who were willing to be warriors.

First, we will review the story of Gideon and the Midianites, then expose the strongman, and outline our strategy. This is what both Esther and Nehemiah did; survey their region and situation, expose the evil and the evil plans, and then fight against it with the strategy that God gives them.

Let's look at the story of Gideon and the Midianties to find what the Lord might be speaking to us today.

Gideon and the Midianites

Even though God delivered the Israelites out of Egyptian bondage and slavery and caused them to flourish and live in peace, they eventually forgot about the goodness of God and lived in rebellion towards Him. In the book of Judges, the Israelites had peace within their borders, but they did evil in the sight of the Lord. For this reason, God allowed the Midianites and other nations to come in and plunder the Israelites of all their increase of crops, produce, and livestock leaving them to starve in the winter. This continued for seven years until the Israelites finally decided to pray and ask God to forgive them. This began the restoration process.

If my people, which are called by my name, shall humble themselves, and pray, and seek my face, and turn from their wicked ways; then will I hear from heaven, and will forgive their sin, and will heal their land.
2 Chronicles 7:14, KJV

31

As in the Days of Midian

Gideon, Called by an Angel

Because the people began to repent and cry out to God for help, He sent the prophet, Gideon, son of Josh, to tell the people why they were in trouble and what they had to do to stop this cycle of robbery by the Midianites. Now, Gideon came from a poor family, and saw himself very small, and the least in his family. Yet, the angel of the Lord who appeared to Gideon referred to Gideon as a "mighty man of valor." Gideon had to shift something in his thinking because he saw himself as small, but the angel of the Lord told Gideon that he was a mighty man of valor. It is not always easy to change the way we see ourselves to the way that God sees us. It is only through reading scripture and having relationship with God that we can see ourselves as God does. Reading and studying scripture helps to renew our minds. God also speaks to us in many ways to impart our identity into us. Gideon's identity was a mighty man of valor. This was revealed to Gideon by an angel. God was shifting the way Gideon had been seeing himself, from very small and the least of them, to a mighty man of valor who would lead an army!

The angel of the Lord told Gideon to go in this might and save his people Israel, from the hand of the

Midianites. Gideon not only had to adjust how he saw himself, but now he would have to walk in this new found identity that this angel had revealed to him and had spoken into him.

It was at this time in Biblical history, that the Lord revealed himself as the Prince of Peace to mankind. It was the first time on earth that God had revealed himself this way by saying, "Peace be unto thee; fear not; thou shalt not die."

In the Bible, when God does something for the first time, it sets a precedence of who God is from then on.

When Gideon realized that it was the angel of the Lord, he exclaimed, "Alas, Sovereign Lord! I have seen the angel of the Lord face to face! But the Lord said to him, "Peace! Do not be afraid. You are not going to die." So, Gideon built an altar to the Lord there and called it The Lord is Peace. To this day it stands in Ophrah of the Abiezrites.
Judges 6:22-24, NIV

Altars of Baal Dismantled

The Lord instructed Gideon to dismantle the altars of Baal that were constructed in their land, and to cut down the Asherah grove of trees that were next to it. This was

33

As in the Days of Midian

where idols were worshipped and sacrificed. The altar of Baal was where human sacrifices were offered, mostly of infants and young children. Abortion clinics today are compared to altars of Baal. Human sacrifice is the worship of false gods no matter when or where it is done. Groves are places where religious worship to false gods took place. This was forbidden to the Israelites and to believers in Jesus Christ. An Asherah was a wooden image of a sensual Canaanite goddess, usually set up in a grove of trees to be worshipped. Gideon destroyed these ungodly altars of pagan worship. Before the Lord could direct and lead Gideon in how to stop the cycle of the Midianites from plundering the Israeli people of their crops, produce, and animals, he had to remove the false religious worship in their land. When there is sin in our lives, the enemy has a right to come in and steal, kill, and destroy from us because we have opened a door giving him a legal right. Removing the idol worship cleansed the land of the power of these false gods. This needed to be done before the Lord would send Gideon out to battle assuring him victory.

Gideon's Army of 300

God told Gideon to call all of Israel together and that they would deliver the people. So, Gideon blew his trumpet and 32,000 men responded. There were 300,000 Midianites and other nations against Israel's 32,000. God told Gideon to send the ones home that were fearful and 22,000 of them went home, leaving 10,000 warriors. Then God told Gideon to take the 10,000 men down to the river and those who get down on both hands and knees to drink were to be sent home, but those who watched for the enemy while lapping like a dog; Gideon was to take them aside. Those who drank on both hands and knees were not being watchful or alert and they were sent home. Only 300 that lapped like a dog remained. That left 300 Israelites to go against 300,000 Midianites and other nations against Israel. With these impossible odds, if Israel won against such a large number of enemies with their very few, which God said they would, they would have no doubt that they did not win in their own strength, but it had to be because God was with them.

God instructed Gideon to divide the 300 men into three companies and put a trumpet in every man's hand,

and an empty pitcher with a lamp inside in the other hand. As Gideon's small army surrounded the enemy's camp, they each blew their trumpet and smashed their glass pitcher causing every Midianite to flee on foot in terror. Gideon's army did win because God fought for them. They only had to be courageous and show up for the battle, but they did not have to fight.

Unlike Gideon, our war is a spiritual battle. We are a spirit being, we live in a body, and we have a soul. We live in a natural world and do not normally see demons or angels. It is a completely different kind of a battle when we fight against an unseen enemy. A spiritual battle is of a different kind. We need to know what weapons are available to us and how to use them. God gave Gideon weapons that seemed foolish, but this divine strategy worked and they overcame their enemies even though they were greatly out numbered.

We must win our battles in the spirit realm, before our victory can manifest in the natural. Not a soul is saved, or a miracle worked, unless somebody prays and battles it through in the spirit realm first. We need to win battles in the spirit realm first by obeying God's instructions and putting all our trust in Him.

The Midianites

Midian was the son of Abraham by Keturah. The Midianites were his descendants.

> *Then again Abraham took a wife and her name was Keturah. And she bare him Zimran and Jokshan and Medan and Midian and Ishbak and Shuah. And Jokshan begat Sheba and Dedan. The sons of Dedan were Asshurim and Letushim and Leummim. And the sons of Midian; Ephah, Epher, Hanoch, Abidah and Eldaah. All these were the children of Keturah.*
> Genesis 25:1-4, KJV

The Midians were an immoral people who vexed others with their wiles and then beguiled them. Wile is a devious or cunning strategy to manipulate or persuade someone to do what he wants them to do. Synonyms are schemes, maneuvers, cunning strategies, and devices. Beguile is to charm, enchant, in a deceptive way, to captivate, bewitch, spellbind, hypnotize, mesmerize, seduce, entice, entrap.

As in the Days of Midian

And the name of the Midianite woman that was slain was Cozbi the daughter of Zur; he was head over a people and of a chief house in Midian. And the Lord spoke unto Moses saying, Vex the Midianites and smite them. For they vex you with their wiles wherewith they have beguiled you in the matter of Peor and in the matter of Cozbi the daughter of a prince of Midian their sister which was slain in the day of the plague for Peor's sake.
Numbers 25:18, KJV

The Midianites identified with the Ishmaelites because the Midianites had bought Joseph and taken him out of the pit, but only to sell him again to the Ishmaelites. This is human slavery, even human trafficking, and an abusive oppression.

So, when the Midianite merchants came by his brothers, they pulled Joseph up out of the cistern and sold him for twenty shekels of silver to the Ishmaelites, who took him to Egypt.
Genesis 37:28, NIV

The Midianites joined Moab in cursing the Israelites through divination. Divination is a form of witchcraft that perverts a person's gifting, call, and identity into a false prophet. Their purpose was to deceive and manipulate. The prophet Balaam was called upon by the elders of both Moab and Midian to curse Israel. The Midianites tempted

38

Balaam to sin against the Israelites. The Midianites seduced Israel. To seduce means to *entice (someone) into sexual activity or attract in a powerful manner to a belief or into a course of action that is inadvisable or foolhardy*. The Midianites sacrificed unto the god of the Midianites who was Baal-peor. To worship and sacrifice to another god other than the one true God Almighty, creator of the universe is whoredom.

And Moab said unto the elders of Midian, Now shall this company lick up all that are round about us as the ox licks up the grass of the field. And Balak the son of Zippor was king of the Moabites at that time. He sent messengers therefore unto Balaam the son of Beor to Pethor which is by the river of the land of the children of his people to call him saying, Behold there is a people come out from Egypt; behold, they cover the face of the earth and they abide over against me. Come now therefore I pray thee, "curse" me this people for they are too mighty for me; peradventure I shall prevail that we may smite them and that I may drive them out of the land, for I know that he whom thou blessed is blessed and he whom thou curses is cursed. And the elders of Moab and the elders of Midian departed with the rewards of divination in their hand and they came unto Balaam and spoke unto him the words of Balak.
Numbers 22:4-7, KJV

As in the Days of Midian

And Israel abode in Shittim and the people began to commit whoredom with the daughters of Moab. And they called the people unto the sacrifices of their gods and the people did eat and bowed down to their gods.
Numbers 25:1-18, KJV

In Gideon's day the Midianites were so powerful in that region that the Israelites were forced to abandon their fields and take shelter in mountain clefts, caves, and strongholds. Together with the Edomite tribe of the Amalekites, they harassed the Israelites as far to the west as the Philistine city of Gaza. The Israelites reportedly suffered at the hands of the Midianites for a period of six years. Midianite raiders destroyed crops and reduced them to extreme poverty.

Then the Israelites did evil in the sight of the Lord and the Lord gave them into the hand of Midian for seven years. The (powerful) hand of Midian prevailed against Israel. Because of Midian the sons of Israel made for themselves the dens (hideouts) which were in the mountains and the caves and the (mountain) strongholds. So, Israel was greatly impoverished because of the Midianties and the Israelites cried out to the Lord for help.
Judges 5:1-2, 6, AMP

The allied army of Midianites and Amalekites encamped in the valley of Jezreel after crossing the Jordan.

40

Now all the Midianites, Amalekites and other eastern peoples joined forces and crossed over (the Jordan) and camped in the Valley of Jezreel.
Judges 6:33, AMP

After having crossed the Jordan. Gideon with his army encamped by the Fountain of Harod, and the Midianite army was located to the north. With 300 men, Gideon succeeded in surprising and routing them and the Midianites fled homeward across the Jordan in confusion. (Judges 7:1-24) Midian is not mentioned again in the Hebrew Bible.

Characteristics of Midianites

- Midianite means, dissension, quarrel, strife, contention, and discord.
- Vex; make you feel annoyed, frustrated, worried, anger, inflamed, enraged, exasperated.
- Wiles: devious, cunning strategies to manipulate, persuade someone to do what he wants.
- Beguiled; charm, enchant, deceptive, captivate, bewitch, spellbind, hypnotize, mesmerize.
- Midianites will vex you with their wiles and cause you to be beguiled.
- The Midianites called Israel to sacrifice to their gods so they ate and bowed down to them.

41

As in the Days of Midian

- When Israel had planted crops, the Midianites came up and destroyed their harvest.
- They left no sustenance; not sheep, ox, or ass, but entered the land to destroy it.
- They purchased Joseph for a slave. Oppressive, abusive, slavery, human trafficking.
- The people (Israel) began to commit whoredom with the Midianites.
- The Midianites will lick up all that is around you, as the ox licks up the grass of the field.
- Arm yourselves unto war and go against the Midianites.

Next, let's look at what the yokes of slavery are, the heavy burdens, and the oppressor's rod.

Slavery, Heavy Burdens, and the Oppressor's Rod

In this scripture, I believe God is speaking over the Northern Red River Valley Territory, telling us what He is going to do; *break the yoke of our slavery, lift the heavy burdens from off of our shoulders, and break the oppressor's rod*. It will be helpful to understand what these are.

> *For You (Lord God) will break the yoke of their slavery and lift the heavy burden from off of our shoulders. You (Lord God) will break the oppressor's rod, just as You did when You destroyed the army of Midian.*
> Isaiah 9:4, NLT

Yoke of Slavery

A yoke according to Webster's American 1828 Dictionary of the English Language is defined as; *a piece of timber, hollowed or made curving near each end, and fitted with bows for receiving the necks of oxen; by which means two are connected for drawing. From a ring or hook in the*

43

bow, a chain extends to the thing to be drawn, or to the yoke of another pair of oxen behind. It is a mark of servitude; slavery; bondage. To enslave; to bring into bondage.[3]

This definition of a yoke being placed on oxen or horses for the purpose of tilling the ground and planting was not meant for harm, but for the cultivation and harvesting of foods. But there were also cruel yokes placed on animals and humans for the purpose of slavery and bondage. In the days of Moses, the Israelites were enslaved by the Egyptians to make bricks out of clay and straw for 430 years. This was an example of a yoke of slavery upon a people.

When people marry one another, they are said to be yoked together, which means they have entered into covenant with each other. This is an example of a godly yoke made by a spoken word or written agreement, which is a covenant of love for each other.

On February 4, 2023, Prophet Bill Lackie shared his Word of the Lord. He shared what God had given to him about a yoke. He stated, "The reason why there is a yoke is because in the Garden of Eden God intended for us to be his fellowship. There was no lack of closeness. He came and walked with Adam and Eve in the cool of the day. And the problem that happened after the Garden of Eden was that man had a lack of God. And in our society, people get addicted, and they go to things that are not of God, that God doesn't want them to do. These are substitutes because we have a void inside of us that God doesn't fill. So, when the anointing comes and fills that void and continually fills that void, there is no need for addictions, no need for escape and no need for entertainment."[4]

God intended for a yoke to be a form of protection and a communion with Him and with one another. Human beings were meant to be relational and connected to God as their father, and to others in loving kind relationships. The Israelites and even some of the Egyptians were saved and led out of bondage only by having the blood of the lamb applied to the doorpost of their homes.

When we are born-again, we come out of Egypt signifying that we were slaves held in bondage, but are now free because the blood of Jesus breaks the yoke of slavery off us. But we must learn to walk and live in that freedom, no longer as slaves to fear, anger, pride, or whatever ungodly attribute we had in Egypt.

I am the Lord your God who brought you out of Egypt so that you would no longer be slaves to the Egyptians, I broke the bars of your yoke and enabled you to walk with heads held high.

Leviticus 26:13, NIV

Heavy Burdens

Burden in the Strong's Concordance #5445 means; *to bear, carry, sustain, to be heavy laden, to drag oneself along.*

During a generational ministry zoom session with Aslan's Place many things in my heritage were identified, one was an "inappropriate burden."[5] Aslan's Place identified this "inappropriate burden" as coming in through my ancestral involvement in freemasonry. This brought the curse of a heavy burden upon the shoulders of those in my generational lineage. The people in this ministry session prayed to cancel that curse through the blood of Jesus. This curse manifested in the natural realm through all three of my children fracturing their collar bones. My first child's collar bone was fractured during birth, my second child at 18 months fell out of his highchair hitting against the edge of a vanity causing his collar bone to fracture, and my third child fractured his collar bone on the school playground in third grade when another child ran into him. I believe the Lord was showing me that the breaking of all three of my children's collar bones was the manifestation of a curse caused by oaths and vows spoken in freemasonry.

This curse continues through our own involvement in occult-type sins. Many times, we do not realize we are involved in occult things because it is so prevalent in our culture. Some examples of activities of occult include, celebrating and participating in Halloween, many movies and video games, and books such as Harry Potter.

The collar bone provides structure for our body and is responsible to carry the weight of the body. Curses that come from involvement in Freemasonry cause actual heavy burdens that weigh upon us. The breaking of the collar bone began in the spiritual realm through spoken word curses and then manifested in the natural realm. Those who are involved in Freemasonry are also making covenant with the gods of Freemasonry during their ceremonies. So, not only do the curses need to be broken, but the ungodly covenants need to be repented of and nullified by a more powerful blood, which is the blood of Jesus Christ. Many sicknesses and diseases are also caused this way, beginning in the spirit realm by negative spoken words and then manifest in the natural realm with harmful diagnosis.

The Oppressor's Rod

Oppressor in the Strong's Concordance #5065 means; *to be a slave driver or a taskmaster*. Rod is #7626 means; *a stick used in walking, discipline, and guidance.*

The oppressor's rod denotes oppression and servitude. The oppressor's rod was like that of Egypt, where the taskmasters or oppressors drove the people to hard labor with a rod.

Midian's defeat represents the breaking of this yoke of slavery, removing the heavy burden from the shoulders, and breaking off the oppressor rod from the people in that region.

God is Raising Up an Army

Quoting Bishop Hamon during this City Tour to the people said, "Now compare this story of Gideon to this region. We here would be just a few people. There has never been a place in the Bible where God said you don't have enough people, but he did tell one man you have too many. God said that is just the right number. 300 against

As in the Days of Midian

300,000. They won because God fought for them. The Lord of Hosts Sabaoth, which means the God of the heavenly armies. War is the element of prayer that is missing."[6]

I believe God is saying that in the Northern Red River Valley Territory, there has been a yoke of slavery, heavy burdens, and an oppressive rod upon the people and that He is raising up an army to go to war with Him to release signs, wonders, and miracles through this army to begin setting the people free.

Now let's look at the this first strongman Freemasonry that was identified during this City Tour.

As in the Days of Midian

.

The Strongman of Freemasonry

Demons exist on three levels. First, there are the ground level demons, which are the lower-level demons that carry out orders from satan's hierarchy to harass and afflict people. These are the kind we can easily see manifest around us and can easily command to leave us. Secondly, there are occult demons that are more hidden and are more organized in how they carry out their evil plans in families and in a region. Third is the highest level of demons, which are principalities and powers in heavenly places that rule over territories and nations. These are like the generals in satan's army. Satan has a hierarchical structure in his kingdom of darkness just as our natural military has its structure of generals, sergeants, captains and then the footmen.

Under this first strongman Freemasonry noted by the City Tour team, two other principalities can be categorized along with it because they are closely related. The three components of this stronghold include the following.

- Freemasonry

As in the Days of Midian

- Leviathan (represented by an alligator or crocodile-looking spirit)
- Jezebel along with all her whoredoms.

Freemasonry

My generational history on my father's side was well documented in books.. Reading in this family history book, I recognized my great, great grandfather's funeral was masonic. It stated he had a masonic funeral and that a sprig leaf was placed on top of his chest signifying eternal life. The sprig of acacia plays a central part in the 3rd and 14th degree ritual of a Freemason and is sometimes laid in graves or on caskets at Masonic funerals. Freemasons borrowed the imagery of the acacia sprig as a symbol of the birth and death mother goddess Neith of ancient Egypt. The acacia is said to have been used in the building of the tabernacle of the Ark of the Covenant. Some Freemasons claim that the crown that Jesus Christ wore at his crucifixion was made of acacia thorns and his cross made of acacia wood, as part of their bizarre attempt to prove that Jesus Christ was himself a "Famous Freemason!" This is part of the deception of Freemasonry. But the truth is that Freemasonry is a religion of witchcraft.

I was always aware that my great grandfather had attended a lodge called the Independent Order of Odd Fellows, a Freemasonry lodge and that my aunts belonged to the Eastern Star, a women's masonic order of masons. I knew both the men and women in my generational lineage had been involved in some form of Freemasonry for several, if not many generations.

In studying Freemasonry, I found vows that people swear by when they join these masonic orders. These vows speak death over their life and the lives of their family. These vows and oaths make covenants with the many demonic gods and goddesses of Freemasonry. Speaking these ungodly vows release curses on the person and their family members. This subjects the people in these families to all kinds of evil things, such as sicknesses, premature death, abandonment, rejection, all types of abuse, sexual perversions, mental weaknesses, addictions to drugs, sex, alcohol, anger, rage, control, manipulation, emotional dependence due to fear, idolatry, poverty, child neglect, pride, religiosity, rebellion, witchcraft, the occult, and division and strife within their families.

As in the Days of Midian

I discovered some reasons for some of the difficulties I experienced because of what I learned about my generational bloodline. To my knowledge, no one in any of my family or generations before me had ever prayed to break these curses off our lives or off any of our descendants; therefore, these curses continued to come upon us and upon our children.

After I got saved by giving my heart to Jesus and making Him my Lord, I realized that during my childhood I had participated in occult rituals releasing and perpetrating the continuation of demonic activity in me and in my life. At holiday gatherings, some of my cousins and I were taught to levitate by an older cousin. We levitated full-grown people from sitting and lying positions. We were only small girls between the ages of 9 and 11 years old. This levitation ritual only worked if we remained sober, that is, without laughing. I remember some of the words to these rituals and recognize these as a form of mocking the death, burial, and resurrection of Jesus Christ.

We did not know it was wrong at the time we were taught these things and participating in them. Our parents, evidently, did not realize they were wrong either. To me it did seem kind of on the dark side; yet we were in a house

full of family enjoying fun and food together. The
levitation we were doing was during family celebration.

Several of my cousins and I also played with a
Ouija board. We asked this Ouija board questions about
people in our family and their future. These are occult
practices. We were taught these from a cousin who was
older than us, who was probably taught from someone
older than them. These practices are passed down from one
generation to the next. The Bible says occult practices are
forbidden and they bring curses upon people who
participate in them.

> *When you enter the land the Lord your God is giving
> you, do not learn to imitate the detestable ways of the
> nations there. Let no one be found among you who
> sacrifices his son or daughter in the fire (abortion), who
> practices divination or sorcery, interprets omens, engages
> in witchcraft, or casts spells, or who is a medium or
> spiritist or who consults the dead. Anyone who does these
> things is detestable to the Lord, because of these same
> detestable practices the Lord your God will drive out those
> nations before you. You must be blameless before the Lord
> your God.*
> Deuteronomy 18:9-13, NIV

As in the Days of Midian

After I gave my life to the Lord and attended a good Bible study, I realized it was wrong for me to participate in levitation, occult rituals, and play with the Ouija Board. This was when I learned there are demonic spirits attached to these types of practices. We make ourselves vulnerable to evil spirits when we participate in these forbidden things.

I did go before the Lord to repent of my involvement in levitation, Ouija Board, handwriting analysis, and reading of horoscopes. I asked God to free me of any demonic association with the occult, so any demon associated with these practices would be removed from my life completely. When we repent, God hears us and forgives us immediately. I whole-heartedly sought God to be free of all evil and wrong things in me. I wanted to know the truth about how to know God and have relationship with Him.

God warns us to stay away from occult practices because they will cause us problems. Sin in our lives affects not only us, but our children and our grandchildren, for several generations. If each generation participates in the same sins, these curses continue that much longer in our generations.

It is wise to be submitted to a body of believers who function in the knowledge of deliverance and who have a Holy Spirit led intercessory group.

Do not defile yourselves in any of these ways, because this is how the nations that I am going to drive out before you became defiled. Even the land was defiled; so, I punished it for its sin, and the land vomited out its inhabitants.
Leviticus 18:24-25, NIV

Freemasons will not specifically ask people to join their organization but go in a round-about way to get the person to ask to join. This person then opens the door themselves giving the devil a legal right to him. There are multiple initiations with ungodly oaths and vows that they are led to speak which unknowingly brings curses upon that person and upon their family. These vows and oaths also bring them into covenant with other gods. Often there is some form of shedding of blood that seals those covenants. Not only do we need to break the curses but the covenants also.

In 2008 I became aware that there were Freemasonry curses working in me and in my family. There was much upheaval in my life and around me that just was not the normal difficulties people experience. I sought God for help and found teaching and deliverance prayers from Bill Sudduth Ministries (https://www.ramministries.org) through their books and media material.[7]

Later I attended conferences where they conducted corporate deliverance prayers to break curses off us, off our whole family and generational lines at several gatherings. One was in Bismarck, North Dakota, another at Redeeming Love church in Minneapolis, and through a group of people gathered in Moorhead, Minnesota. I also attended a weeklong training at Francis and Judith McNutt in Jacksonville, Florida to specifically renounce all effects of Freemasonry in me and in my generational lineage.

When people make oaths, vows, promises, and covenants with organizations, they become partakers of what is associated with that organization. These promises and oaths were made to the many gods of Freemasonry and brought with them curses that continued to come upon each generation bringing sickness, poverty, accidents, premature death, strife, and all kinds of problems. These covenants and curses become burdensome yokes and heavy weights and rods of oppression put on us that God never intended for us to have.

These covenants and curses can be broken through the blood of Jesus. We can pray for each other and our families to have these generational covenants and curses removed from us so we can be healed. The blood of Jesus is the only thing that has the power to break a demonic curse and remove the burden of sin and oppression. Once we become personally free of sin and the resulting curses, we can pray for our families to know the love of God so they can also be restored also. Our homes were meant to be places of safety and security.

This is missing in families where there is involvement in Freemasonry. The difficulties that these generational curses create can cause people to give up hope; or they can propel people to run to God for help.

When we are born-again our spirit is made brand new and comes alive unto God. When we are filled with the Holy Spirit we are empowered and given gifts to be a witness, but our soul still needs to be sanctified. That is why it is important to uproot any Freemasonry vow, breaking off any curse so the life of God can begin to flow in us and into our children's lives.

Five Categories of Freemasonry Curses

- Curses inherited by our forefathers and mothers cause generational curses and iniquitous patterns. Sins of our ancestors affect the children to the 3rd and the 4th generations. Some things we deal with aren't anything we did but is in our bloodline causing us to have a weakness toward certain sins.[8]
- Words we speak over our ourselves and others become curses. Words we speak have power. Our words speak life or death over ourselves and over others.[9]
- Broken vow curses come through a broken vow to God or man such as marriage vows that are broken. When people do not understand the importance of making a covenant, they do not realize they may bring a curse upon their lives when they break it. The devil hates Godly marriages and will try to destroy them, bringing harm to your children.[10]
- Some curses come from people who practice witchcraft and sorcery. A witch can speak a curse upon a person or home, but a believer in Christ has power to break it off through the name of Jesus. Believers should pray prayers of protection because there is an evil power in witchcraft that comes from the devil.[11]
- The consequences of our own sin can manifest in the form of curses. When we sin, we give the devil a legal right to torment us. We open a door in the spirit realm and the devil steps in and gets a foothold. If we continue in sin; a foothold becomes a stronghold.[12]

All five of these curses could be working in our lives depending on our involvement or our family's involvement in Freemasonry. Some orders of Freemasonry include: Independent Order of Odd Fellows, Women's Order of Eastern Star, DeMolay, Rainbow Girl, Woodmen of the North, Knights of Columbus, Shriners, and the Rebekah's.

If you were involved in these, you can have all five of these curses working in your life. If you weren't involved, but your family was you can have three of those curses in your life. That is a lot of unseen things working against you. If you are English, Irish, Scottish, German, Norwegian, French, Spanish, African American in your bloodline; you have Freemasonry working in your family.[13]

Four Fruits of Freemasonry
Asthma and Allergies

In the First Degree of Freemasonry initiation, a noose is put around the initiates' neck and they are symbolically choked. Because the initiate agrees to have this done, he welcomes a curse of breathing problems to come upon him and his generational lineage. This curse will cause breathing problems in the throat and chest and restrict their voice from being heard. During these initiations, confessions and vows are made to the many gods of Freemasonry, which looses demonic spirits into people's lives. These demonic spirits can cause sicknesses such as asthma and allergies because the evil spirit is assigned to stop the breath in some way. This particular vow or oath will need to be renounced in order to break the curse off of the person's life and generational lineage.[14]

Declaration to Break the Curse

I repent for my ancestors (and myself if involved) for participating in this 1st degree of Freemasonry. And for making vows and oaths to all of these Freemasonry gods. I renounce the noose around my neck and my ancestor's necks, and the fear of choking and every spirit causing asthma, hay fever, allergies, emphysema of other breathing difficulties. I pray for the healing and restoration of my throat, my vocal cords, my nasal passages, sinuses, bronchial tubes, and for the healing of my speech area and the release of the Word of God into me and through me.

Perversions and Molestations

This is a curse caused by sexual abuse that can occur at any age. It is a curse that was invoked by a Freemason in our family and it opened a door for sexual abuse to come in at some point in the descendants' lives. This perversion also perverts our voice and what we speak. It comes in through a spirit of perversion working in us by an inherited curse. This perversion is in our bloodline and wants to hide but needs to be exposed. When we speak to someone, our words may become perverted or twisted by the time, they are received.[15] This happens because there is a curse of perversion at work. This curse can be broken by repenting for our own involvement in occult and for our family's involvement in Freemasonry and then by renouncing the vow that was spoken. This removes the legal right given to the enemy to afflict us. After this curse is removed, that space in us needs to be filled with the truth of the Word and the Holy Spirit. This is done by receiving Jesus Christ into our lives and receiving the Baptism of the Holy Spirit and by continuing to study scripture. The evil spirit will look for an opportunity to come back, but we must guard our hearts by remaining in the Word and praying in the Holy Spirit.

Anger

This anger is a rage empowered by a demonic spirit and not a normal typical anger. It boils over causing harm to others. There is no control over this anger which can prompt physical and verbal harm to another person. This is the kind of anger that can manifest in a person causing a stroke or heart attack. It gets set-off very quickly and unexpectedly causing a person not think or act in a humanly manner.[16]

Fear

This is a spirit of fear and has rule over what we do and speak. It causes panic to paralyze us. This spirit affects the hypothalamus and amygdala part of the brain overloading the nervous system. This can be seen when someone is jittery and has physical manifestations of nervousness.[17] The amygdala processes fear, sending signals to the hypothalamus to trigger a fight or flight response.

The hypothalamus keeps the body systems in balance by affecting the heart rate and respirations to prepare for action if perceived. Stimuli from the environment is sent to the amygdala, signaling the hypothalamus to react, or respond to the stimuli.

A spirit of fear influences us in an irrational manner. We must set a guard of God's peace over our heart and mind by developing an intimate relationship with the Lord, reading the Word, and praying in Spirit.

And the peace of God which surpasses all understanding will guard your hearts and minds through Christ Jesus.
Philippians 4:7, NKJV

A Mason will say they belong to a do-good organization, but it is a religion. There are masonic bibles on an altar in a Freemason's temple. The Shriner's hospital does care for crippled children and burn victims, but it is based on Freemasonry principles. Masons do many good things in communities, but it is for earning their way to a celestial peace in eternity. They are well-funded and organized.

As in the Days of Midian

Martha Lucia, who was a Christian International minister, and author, noted that her son was in a Shriner's hospital after receiving burns to much of his body. She stated they gave good care to her son, but noted her son had a rebellion in him that was not there before being admitted to their hospital. She felt a spirit of rebellion was imparted to him while at the Shriner's hospital. She stated that though his body was healed, he came home a different person after having been there.[18]

The biggest lie of Freemasonry is; "Man is not sinful he is merely imperfect and can redeem himself through good works."

That is not what a Christian Bible says.

For all have sinned and fall short of the glory of God.
Romans 3:23, NIV

Inside a Freemason bible it talks about the "Great Light of Freemasonry." This is a mixing of truth and is an error in this religion. It is difficult for a person who has been in Freemasonry to walk in freedom after they truly become saved because of the many yokes of bondage that are placed upon them. It is also difficult for someone who has Freemasonry in their family background to accept the

66

grace that God offers and that they do not need to perform to be good enough. That is a religious spiritual stronghold. When we do not get delivered of the mixture of the profanity in Freemasonry, it will pull us out of the grace of our relationship with Christ, like losing our first love without knowing it happened. The wrong things in us will stay in us until we get rid of them. They will have a negative effect on our relationship with the Lord if we don't deal with them and get delivered of them and replace it with the truth.

The Masonic bible has the all-seeing Eye, Horus the Egyptian god, the compass, the square, the G, the Scottish and York Rites and this is mixing the holy and the profane.

If we are born again and even spirit filled and have Freemasonry in our family background there can still be a mixture if these curses have not been repented of and have not been renounced. This brings a spirit of error, a perverse spirit, and a lying spirit into a descendant of Freemasonry. This can be broken by recognizing the sin and error in Freemasonry, repenting of it and renouncing it all through the blood of Jesus Christ and then by walking it out in truth and purity.

As in the Days of Midian

Let's repent of Freemasonry and then pray to break specific curses and covenants of generational infirmities. Some of these could include: bone cancer, heart problems, diabetes, dementia, etc. We will pray a general prayer together and insert the specific infirmity from which we or our family need healing.

Prayer—Repent and Renounce Freemasonry

In the name of Jesus Christ, I hereby reject and renounce any involvement in or association with or any heritage of the Masonic religion. I reject everything about it and cut it off me and off my family in the name of Jesus Christ. Father God, in Jesus' name, I ask You to forgive me and my ancestors for our involvement in any of the various branches of the Masonic religion. I repent of praying to or communicating with any of these deities or to any of their mythical personalities. I repent of taking any secret vow or oath. I repent of invoking or agreeing with any curses upon myself or my family. I repent of covenanting with any and all gods of Freemasonry and set my heart to follow You Lord God and to represent You and Jesus as best that I can. I declare that because I have repented and renounced all Freemasonry activity in my life and my family's lives there is no more legal right for any curse or ungodly covenant of Freemasonry to be at work in my life. Holy

68

Spirit, lead me into all truth. Thank You, Father.

Prayer to Break Curses

Father, I thank You that the blood of Jesus is active, powerful, and able to break any curse that is working in my life and the lives of my family. Father, I recognize that many in my family have problems with _____ (name the infirmity that is common in your family). Therefore, I recognize, according to Your Word, that there must have been an open door of sin that allowed this to come into my family and has been passed down in my generations. I do not know where this occurred in my ancestors, but I repent on behalf of my ancestors, for the sin that was committed that allowed this curse to perpetuate in my family and in my generational lineage.

Father, You said that Jesus became a curse for us in Galatians 3:13, so we do not have to be cursed. I do not want any sinful ways in my life. Show me any area in my life that is not right so that I may change it. Father, You gave us authority to command sickness and anything that is not of You to leave our bodies. So, in the name of Jesus and through the power of the blood of Jesus, I break the curse of _____ off me and off my family. I draw a line

As in the Days of Midian

right here, right now with the blood of Jesus, and say that curse must stop today. I declare that no more curse or sickness can come upon me and my family. I break its power by applying the blood of Jesus. All demons associated with the curse of _____ and death, I command you to leave me and my family now, in Jesus' name. You no longer have any legal right to us. Go now in Jesus' name, and I speak healing to my family and me in Jesus' name, Amen!

Leviathan/Alligator/Crocodile

Although there are many gods worshipped in Freemasonry, Baphomet is the main god. Its upper body is a man, and its lower body is that of a goat. The occult pentagram is often shown with a goat's head inside of this five-pointed star and letters surrounding it that say, "I am Lucifer." The satanic bible defines this pagan god as Baphomet, a fallen angel. In Isaiah 14, satan was the fallen angel.

*How you have fallen from heaven, morning star, son of the
dawn! You have been cast down to the earth, you who once
laid low the nations! You said in your heart, "I will ascend
to the heavens; I will raise my throne above the stars of
God' I will sit enthroned on the mount of assembly, on the
utmost heights of Mount Zaphon. I will ascend above the
tops of the clouds; I will make myself like the Most High."
But you are brought down to the realm of the dead, to the
depths of the pit.*

Isaiah 14:12-15, NIV

Yvonne Kitchen writes in her book *Freemasonry,
Death in the Family,* "the occult pentagram is often shown
with a goat's head within the five-pointed star, and letters
surrounding it: I am Lucifer. Those letters, when read
clockwise and starting from the bottom read LEVYThN,
the Hebrew spelling of Leviathan, the female sea monster
of Job 41. Again, the female face of Lucifer himself."[19]

The pentagram represents the five elements of
witchcraft: air, earth, fire, water, and spirit. All five of these
elements are represented in this god of Freemasonry. Air is
represented by Baphomet's wings. Fire is at the top of
Baphomet's head. He is pictured sitting on the earth, which
is surrounded by water. This idol god is part human and
part animal; part man and part female, therefore causes

As in the Days of Midian

confusion in those under its influence regarding their sexuality and identity; a double mindedness.

Such a person is double-minded and unstable in all they do.
James 1:8, NIV

God speaks to us in dreams to warn us and to help us to know how to pray. So, when I had a dream of an alligator, I knew that had to be God speaking to me because having lived in the Midwest most of my life, an alligator is not common in our environment and not ever something I would experience. God wanted to give me some revelation so I could pray more effectively.

Dream, January 28, 2017
I had a dream that I was standing in my living room when I saw a very large alligator walk right in front of me. It came through a door into our living room, walked in front of me going into the kitchen, and exiting a door on the other side of this kitchen. It didn't stop or hesitate, but boldly and quickly strutted through our entire house. In the kitchen was a 2-year-old baby crawling around on the floor. This alligator walked right by this baby without seemingly even noticing it or harming the child. Yet, I was really concerned for this baby because I knew the alligator was

evil and only had harmful intention in my home and for that baby. I was alarmed when I saw it in the house. Then I heard the voice of my family in the house say, "Oh, he will not hurt anyone. He is a pet. Do not worry. He is welcome to come into our house." They were referring to the alligator. Everything inside of me rose-up in alarm because I knew that was not the truth. The other people in the house thought this alligator was a pet, something like what a dog would be, but I knew that the alligator was a grave danger to all of us, especially the 2-year-old baby. In one snap of his mouth that baby would be devoured. We would need to get the alligator out of the house immediately and keep it out.

This is where the dream ended.

In the Bible, the alligator and crocodile are symbolic of Leviathan. In my dream, my family in the house said this was a pet and it was okay for this alligator-type creature to be there. They did not discern that danger was right there in the house with us. The book of Job tells us the truth about Leviathan.

Can you make a pet of it like a bird or put it on a leash for the young women in your house?

Job 41:5, NIV

As in the Days of Midian

The baby in my dream signified the little children and blessings in our family lineage. A baby is the most innocent of humans. A baby in a dream can also represent desires and dreams that we carry inside of us waiting to be birthed. It is the things we pray about. A baby can represent the beginning of a ministry or a business we are embarking on. An alligator, crocodile, or Leviathan has no mercy and will attack and devour whatever is in his way, especially those things that God loves.

While attending a prayer group during this time, we discussed alligators in relationship to Leviathan. One prayer member said an alligator represents a family curse. Speaking by revelation he continued to say, the alligator or crocodile is a deadly evil generational spirit! He shared an incident many years ago when his friend had come to college to play football. While getting settled in his apartment, his roommate entered the room. When the roommate entered the room, his friend saw an alligator come into the room with him. When this alligator came into the room, an argument began between the two roommates. This friend, who witnessed seeing the alligator come into the room, knew the alligator had something to do with the arguing and the strife that flared up between them. His friend saw this alligator in the spirit realm, it was not in the natural realm. This is not something we choose to see on our own, but it is God's grace that allows us to see in the spirit realm for the purpose of praying about it, to overcome evil.

At the end of this prayer time, we all had an opportunity to share what we saw and heard from the Lord. One of the people shared that he saw an angel come to each of us, giving us a rolled-up scroll that had personalized answers that we needed for the prayers we prayed that day. The next day while in my quiet time with the Lord, I heard the Lord say, "The rejection people feel within their family is caused by a generational curse of rejecting God. This curse comes through the vows and oaths their ancestors make to other gods."

These ungodly vows and oaths come through involvement in secret society organizations such as Freemasonry, or religious organizations that do not teach the way of salvation through receiving Jesus Christ as their savior nor acknowledge the ministry of the Holy Spirit. The ungodly vows and oaths made in these organizations open the door for demonic spirits to access a person and their

75

family and their generational lineage. When they make vows and oaths to submit their allegiance, time, money, and all they own to another god other than God the Creator of Heaven and Earth, they become a slave to that idol and are in covenant with that god. They no longer are in covenant with Yeshua Hamashiach, the God who loves them and has a purpose for their lives, and who protects them.

That is how the alligator in my dream was allowed to get into my house or into my family lineage. It was a generational curse of Freemasonry. It was given further access by my own participation and involvement through my own words and actions whether knowingly or unknowingly. Alligator spirits devour our dreams and hopes so we cannot fulfill and live out the destinies God has for us. That is what this baby represented in my dream, godly things being birthed in us.

Alligator spirits rob from our families and our businesses so we do not become successful and instead die prematurely or become sick or overcome by poverty. Alligator spirits turn people against each other causing division, separation, strife, divorce, homes out of order, and family feuding. An alligator spirit causes abortion, drug addiction, suicide and anything that kills, steals, and destroys.

We open doors to the alligator spirit when we worship other gods. Most of the time, people are not aware that they are worshipping false gods because of lack of discernment, lack of biblical teaching, and traditional mindsets. When we make these ungodly vows and oaths, we are rejecting our Father God who formed us with His own hands. When we reject God by giving our allegiance to other gods, we allow a curse to come upon us and upon our families. It opens our children up to drug addiction, suicide, premature death, abortion, division, and strife. This will keep going from one generation to the next generation until someone in that family stops it. Someone must become a Christian through receiving Jesus Christ as their savior, become knowledgeable in prayer, and use their authority through Christ Jesus to break that iniquitous pattern through the power of the blood of Jesus Christ.

Leviathan has many heads, and therefore manifests in different ways and in different water-type animal forms. These can all be identified as to how they manifest in a person's life, family, and region. The enemy must be

As in the Days of Midian

identified so that its influence can be dismantled. To identify a head, we only need to look at the characteristics.

It was you who split open the sea by your power; you broke the heads of the monster (dragons) in the waters. It was you who crushed the heads of Leviathan and gave it as food to the creatures of the desert.
Psalm 74:13-14, NIV

The Lord speaks in words or parables encoded with truth. It is the Holy Spirit who decodes these words or parables for those who seek out their meaning. God also uses symbols, signs, or characters to speak to us. God exposes wickedness in humans or spirits, often by referring to animals or birds. The Book of Hosea reveals this method of revelation used by God to instruct His people.[20]

I have also spoken by the prophets, and I have multiplied visions, and used similitudes (symbols), by the ministry of the prophets.
Hosea 12:10, KJV

Barbie Breathitt describes the alligator in her *A to Z Dream Symbology Dictionary* this way. Alligator: large powerful mouth of an envious person in authority telling strong "tales" that are propelled through groups of people; an enemy who is moving below or behind the scene to ruin

78

a person's life, to devour with words that bite to drag their victim down in a death-roll tearing chunks from their flesh then bury them by slander, gossip or verbal abuse; demon or evil spirit influencing an enemy to speak words of accusation; Leviathan – only the Lord has power over it.[21]

Strife and contention are manifestations of Leviathan. One primary means of sowing destruction is to distort perceptions of what has been said causing those under its influence to hear innocent things in a twisted way. People then pass their twisted perceptions on to another person, and it is now cloaked as truth, injecting poison into relationships, and weakening bonds of love and unity.

He shall suck the poison of asps; the viper's tongue shall slay him.
Job 20:16, KJV

Leviathan has an impenetrable armor type body covering. This is symbolic of pride. Strife and contention are fueled by pride. In my dream of the alligator walking through our house I saw an attitude of pride and arrogance that was carried throughout its body. There was no gentleness or kindness or consideration for others. It had more of an attitude of, "I am here, and I have a legal right to be here. You are all my slaves who now serve me. I have a right to everything you own, to use for my own purposes and there is nothing you can do about it." Leviathan is so prideful that he thinks he is above God and deserves our worship.

The truth is when Jesus died on the cross and went to Hell, he destroyed all the works of the devil and delegated all power and authority to His church.

When we repent and renounce ungodly vows and oaths, we remove the legal right that we had previously given to our enemies. Now we can receive God's blessings as we submit ourselves to God's hand of protection and live according to His ways. God will deal with our enemies as we repent and renounce them.

Because of its pride, a Leviathan spirit hates prayer. It is independent and self-sufficient. One who is influenced by this spirit feels they have it all taken care of and does not really need God. It speaks harsh in its communication with God and with people.

By pride comes nothing but strife.
Proverbs 13:10a, NKJV

He who is of a proud heart stirs up strife.
Proverbs 28:25a, NKJV

Another head of Leviathan is his independence and
covenant breaking. It stirs up division, dissension, and
divorce. It offers no grace and stands against the work of
the new covenant of healing, miracles, and speaking in
tongues, and the power of God. It keeps people from
seeking help and from confessing their sins to another. In
God, believers are joined together as one body and must be
interdependent.

Will he make a covenant with you?
Job 41:4a, NKJV

The Strong's Concordance #3882 identifies
Leviathan as: *sea monster, this refers both to a serpent like
sea creature and to a mythological monster of chaos
opposed to the true God; and mourning.*

Leviathan creates chaos leaving a trail of
destruction behind him. He makes his own rules and does
not care about the consequences. He will resist God and
create havoc for the people who love God and desire to be

81

used by God. He hates the moving of the Holy Spirit and the divine leadership of it; therefore it will keep the turmoil of chaos swirling. He will spread sorrow and mourning wherever he goes.

When he raises himself up, the mighty are afraid; Because of his crashing they are bewildered. The sword that reaches him cannot avail. Nor (does) the spear, the dart, or the javelin. He considers iron as straw, Bronze as rotten wood. The arrow cannot make him flee; Slingstones are treated as stubble by him. Clubs are regarded as stubble; He laughs at the rushing and the rattling of the javelins. His underparts are like sharp pieces of broken pottery; He moves across and spreads out (grooves) like a threshing sledge on the mire (muddy riverbanks). He makes the deep water boil like a pot; He makes the sea like a (foaming) pot of ointment. Behind him he makes a shining wake; One would think the deep to be gray-haired (with foam).
Job 41:25-32, AMP

A Leviathan spirit is fortified allowing no one or nothing to penetrate him. He does not care about anyone, but himself. Its hard outer covering of pride will bow to no one. He lives to cause chaos, confusion, and strife wherever he goes.

Who can penetrate or strip off his outer armor? Who can come to his jaws with a double bridle? Who can open the doors (jaws) of his face? Around his (open jaws and) teeth there is terror. His strong scales are his pride, Bound together as with a tight seal. One is so near to another. That no air can come between them. They are joined one to another. They stick together and cannot be separated.
Job 41:13-17, AMP

Leviathan is stiff-necked, and rebellious. According to Websters 1828 Dictionary stiff-necked means, *stubborn, inflexibly obstinate, contumacious (willfully disobedient to authority) as a stiff-necked people; stiff-necked pride.*[22]

In Leviathan's neck resides strength and dismay, and terror dances before him. The folds of his flesh are joined together, Firm on him and immobile (when he moves).
Job 41:22-23, AMP

Being stiff-necked is cruel, grievous, rebellious, and hard. If we desire to flow and move with the Holy Spirit, we must be pliable and flexible, and willing to change, led by the Holy Spirit. In fact, we are to live, and move, and having our whole being in the Holy Spirit.

As in the Days of Midian

For in him we live, and move, and have our being; as also some of your own poets have said, For we are also his offspring.

Acts 17:28, KJV

Leviathan has a heart of stone. When it stocks its prey, it does not turn back or repent or have any mercy. People who are influenced by Leviathan will reject the truth. If they don't understand speaking in tongues or the ministry of deliverance, they come against it without searching it out for themselves or going to God for the answer. Our hearts can become hardened when we do not talk to God, or study the scriptures for understanding, or get our questions answered by God alone. Our hearts become hard when we continue to reject the truth or ask God for help. The longer this goes on, the more difficult it is to hear God's voice.

His heart is as hard as stone. Indeed, as solid as a lower millstone.

Job 41:24, NIV

We can become free of a Leviathan spirit through repentance, renunciation and breaking covenants by oaths and vows to it in Freemasonry using the blood of Jesus

84

Christ to cancel its power to influence us. Our minds can be renewed by the Word of God and our family traditions can change. As we recognize our need for God, we acquire humility and pride is removed from us. By applying God's principles to our lives, we can crucify our flesh removing our old nature. In submitting to God, we resist the devil and have relationship with others in Christ.

Prayer to Repent and Renounce Leviathan

Father, in Jesus' name, I come before You to repent of the pride in my heart and for trying to protect myself from being accountable. I repent for not humbling myself before You and others; for wanting to hide my faults and closing off counsel. I choose to turn away from pride and remove any spirit of self-protection that has limited Your access to my heart. I choose to open my heart to You and to others. Thank You Lord God, for those You have put in my life to hold me accountable. I willingly embrace any needed correction or direction that will further my growth, maturity, and sensitivity to Your work in my life. I renounce the Leviathan spirit of pride in my life and nullify all words and actions that have been prideful, arrogant, and self-serving. According to Ephesians 4:2, I choose to be like Christ in being completely humble and gentle; patient and bearing with others in love. Please continue to show me any ways in which pride may seek to reenter my heart. Thank You for cleansing me by Your blood. In Jesus' name. Amen.

Because Leviathan can be a principality over a region. Believers who have been set free personally, can agree together in prayer over their own territory with corporate authority to seek God for the removal of a Leviathan principality. When led by apostolic leadership within a local congregation, this corporate prayer can be especially powerful in a community or region.

Jezebel and Whoredoms

Jezebel was the daughter of Ethbaal, the king of the Zidonians. She married Ahab who ruled northern Israel from 874-853 BC. Jezebel worshipped Baal and practiced all forms of witchcraft. Ahab allowed all her idol worship and whoredoms to come into that region. This was the first time a king of Israel entered into a marriage with a heathen princess. Because of this, Ahab allowed the worship of pagan gods and the worship of Baal to enter into Israel. Jezebel built numerous temples to the god of Baal, which the Philistines worshiped, and which were against the laws of God. Jezebel made sure her version of religion, idolatry, and witchcraft were honored. Jezebel raised up her own false prophets so her doctrines could go forth in that land. This led the people away from the worship of the One True God Jehovah. Ahab provoked the Lord God of Israel to anger more than all the kings of Israel that were before him.

Queen Jezebel is the representation of all that is evil and against Christ. Jezebel was a real person in 1 Kings 16. Later in the Bible, Jezebel is referred to a spiritual entity who has the same characteristics and attributes of this Jezebel in 1 Kings 16. This spirit influences people in a region to worship the same pagan god Baal and practice all its immorality, manipulations, control, and deceptive ways. Jezebel hates the prophets of God, hates godly leadership, and hates anything that has to do with God.

Jezebel can be traced back to the spirit of Ashtoreth, the chief goddess of the Phoenicians of which Baal was the male counterpart. Jezebel is often referred to as the Queen of Heaven.

As in the Days of Midian

She was the goddess of love and war and associated with fertility. The spirit of Jezebel mocks and perverts God's holiness, purity, and plan to reproduce godly offspring. Her purpose is to draw attention to herself and away from the Holy Spirit. She does this by counterfeiting the Holy Spirit to gain power and exert control. It will never draw one closer to Jesus or to the work of the cross but draws attention to the gift and manifestation of its power. Jezebel was jealous of Elijah's gift and sought to kill him.

The Jezebel spirit often attacks the prophetic vessels who operate in supernatural authority or activity and attempts to kill the prophet. It is the ministry of the prophet that can expose Jezebel, that is why she hates the true prophets of God and legitimate authority.

Jezebel sent a messenger to Elijah to accuse and threaten him. These were curses of witchcraft that caused Elijah to become very oppressed and to run and hide.

So, Jezebel sent a messenger to Elijah to say, "May the gods deal with me, be it ever so severely, if by this time tomorrow I do not make your life like that of one of them." Elijah was afraid and ran for his life.
1 Kings 19:2-3a, NIV

Jezebel exerted influence over authority and manipulated leaders for her own purposes.

So, the elders and nobles who lived in Naboth's city did as Jezebel directed in the letters, he had written to them.
1 Kings 21:11-13, NIV

Jezebel is referenced in the New Testament by the apostle John warning the church of Thyatira, indicating this spirit was working in the church then and is today and should not be tolerated.

As in the Days of Midian

Nevertheless, I have a few things against you, because you allow that woman Jezebel, who calls herself a prophetess, to teach and seduce My servants to commit sexual immorality and eat things sacrificed to idols. And I gave her time to repent of her sexual immorality, and she did not repent. Indeed, I will cast her into a sickbed, and those who commit adultery with her into great tribulation, unless they repent of their deeds. I will kill her children with death, and all the churches shall know that I am He who searches the minds and hearts. And I will give to each one of you according to your works.
Revelation 2:19-23, NKJV

Many who come under the influence of Jezebel struggle with sickness and infirmity, especially if the stronghold is generational. This is part of Jezebel's curse, but can be removed through repentance and turning away from her control, manipulation and the perverted ways that she operates.

Jezebel is the depths of satan and leads to idolatry. She used her occult powers and witchcraft to lure people into idolatry through sexual immorality. Jezebel's occult influence is done in secret and is not easily exposed. Occult means hidden. Her victims are lured by a spirit of seduction into immorality. The children of Israel could not enter the promised land because of their unfaithfulness; their many whoredoms.

And your children shall wander in the wilderness forty years and bear your whoredoms (unfaithfulness) until your carcasses be wasted in the wilderness.
Numbers 14:33, KJV

Yvonne Kitchen has written some books on Freemasonry and brings more understanding of Jezebel's role in that. She says when a woman marries a man who is a mason, she automatically gets a Jezebel mantle because of his operating in a Luciferian priesthood of Baal. It is a Luciferian priesthood of Baal. So, she marries him (Baal) and she is (Jezebel) spiritually speaking.[23]

Jezebel cannot function without an Ahab. This can be in a marriage relationship, a business relationship, or even a working relationship. Ahab was morally weak and religiously tolerant. He allowed Jezebel to worship whoever she wanted, and he participated along with her tolerating all kinds of wickedness. Just as Jezebel and Ahab were after Naboth's vineyard, so are they after our spiritual inheritance. Ahab was self-focused and selfish manipulating Jezebel to take charge of situations and accomplish his agenda. If Jezebel had to murder someone standing in her way, that was not a problem for her. She has no empathy, not even for her own family. This spirit will use, abuse, and manipulate others to get what it wants.

A person who is strongly influenced by a Jezebel spirit will have no empathy for others. Empathy is the ability to understand and share the feelings of another person. It is being able to relate to another human being in words and in actions from a heart position. A Jezebel does not have this character, she is narcissistic. When we do not turn to God with a repented heart attitude, we can become hard-hearted and narcissistic allowing a Jezebel-type spirit to become embedded in our character. A narcissist will keep those who are in relationship with them, in a box with the lid shut tight. The tactics a narcissist uses are: causes insecurity and low self-esteem in its victim, undermine and insult one's personhood, plays mind games of what really happened, uses a push-and-pull/hot-and-cold/idealize-and-discard in their relationships, gaslighting, de-personifying its victim, and sexual temptations and seductions.

As Jezebel spirit devalues a person over time causing them to become insecure and to have a low self-esteem. This is not what God intends for us. God wants us to be secure in who we are and why we are here. Our identity is in Jesus Christ when we give our lives to Him and invite His Spirit to live in us. The Holy Spirit gives us all the fruit of the Spirit, which is love, joy, peace, goodness, kindness, gentleness, self-control, patience, and faith. This is who we are. Our Father God is our protector and our provider. He is our healer and the one who watches over us because we are his beloved children.

A narcissist or Jezebel undermines and insults those they are in relationship with to gain a power over them causing their victim to become their slave. Those insults become a part of the enslaved persons own speech and identity adding to their low self-esteem. Jezebel will keep this control over its victim by an undermining, insulting relationship.

A Jezebel will invoke mind games with its victim. Signs of these include: 1) Never knowing where you stand with them. 2) Questioning yourself often. 3) Many put downs. 4) Turn others against you. 5) Claim you are a liar. 6) Make endless comparisons. 7) Wanting the victim to always come to them. 8) Regularly shuts you out. 9) They never let their guard down. 10) They try to make you jealous. 11) They are secretive. 12) Your gut tells you something is off.[24]

As in the Days of Midian

A Jezebel will push and pull, be hot and cold, and will idealize and discard ones they are in relationship with. It is hard to know what to expect from this person or what kind of a mood they will be in and behavior they will show toward you. This causes confusion in a relationship and a feeling of always being off balance. It is for the purpose of manipulating and controlling.

Gaslighting is the act of undermining another person's reality by denying facts, the environment around them, or other's feelings. Targets of gaslighting are manipulated into turning against their cognition, their emotions, and who they fundamentally are as people. This is an exploitation of their attachment to another. Gaslighting happens in relationships where there is an unequal power dynamic, and the target has given the gas lighter power and often their respect.

A Jezebel de-personifies or mirrors another person, treating another as something other than the unique individual that they really are. It is giving a human the qualities of an inanimate or non-living object. It is a disorder involving feelings of being detached from one's surroundings because of mental confusion.

A Jezebel will lure and seduce through sexual temptation for their own sexual pleasure to include sodomy. oral or anal sex or any kind of sexual perversion. This is not love, it is abuse.

> *My people ask counsel at their stocks and their staff declares unto them: for the spirit of whoredoms hath caused them to err and they have gone a whoring from under their God.*
>
> Hosea 4:12, KJV

Whoredoms

Webster's American 1828 Dictionary defines Whoredom as: *lewdness, fornication, practice of unlawful commerce with the other sex. It is applied to either sex or to any kind of illicit commerce.*[25]

This type of whoredoms has no chastity or faithfulness to abstain from the lust of the flesh. There is no concern for the pain they cause to others in pleasing their own lust, nor do they care about the breaking of the heart of the one they are supposed to be faithful too.

In Webster's American 1828 Dictionary in Scripture Whoredom is defined as: *idolatry, the desertion of the worship of the true God, for the worship of idols.*[26]

As in the Days of Midian

Whoredoms places something higher than God such as time with God or obedience to His word, will, or way. It is an unfaithfulness to God by fulfilling the lust of their flesh. It does not care that selfish actions break the heart of God who was at one time their first love; Christ who gave all for them; His bride.

For I am jealous over you with godly jealousy: for I have espoused you to one (spiritual) husband, that I may present you as a chaste virgin to Christ.
2 Corinthians 11:2, KJV

When the bride of Christ (believers) chose to leave their first love to indulge the lust of the flesh the spirit of whoredom is at work. The entire book of Hosea is a similitude that expresses this sad truth and the anguish it causes to the heart of God. Once we are saved, we become the bride of Christ, but satan is ever tempting the bride to indulge in acts of spiritual whoredom by tempting us with food while fasting, entertainment when God calls us to prayer, seeking attention from people rather than from God, and immoral sinful acts that please the flesh and cause us to turn away from obeying the voice of Christ. Anything that causes us to make a self-pleasing decision that opposes the will and word of our spiritual husband (Christ) is the spirit of whoredom.

It can be broken down to self-rule with no regard for the heart of God whom we hurt every time we choose to lust after our flesh over choosing Him. Just like whoredom in the physical sense breaks the heart of our earthly spouse; in the spiritual sense it shows we truly love ourselves and care about pleasing ourselves more than we love and care to please God. That is a very hurtful place to be.

God is merciful and patient in His cries for us to repent, but if we refuse, He will not stay in that hurtful place indefinitely. It is so hurtful of a situation to God that He would rather forget that He ever knew us than to continue having us call Him our own while pleasing the will of another. If we choose to forget our other lovers such as our idols, sins, and selfish desires, and put our full faith in Him, He will forget our sins and welcome us with open arms. But if we do not turn away from loving the things of the world, He will choose to forget that He ever knew us even if we continue to call ourselves by His name.

It is in the same manner that an adulterous wife might still carry the name of her husband, but through the abundance of adulteries and refusal to walk along side of his kind intentions toward her, she has lost his heart. This was a warning to the church of Thyratria, but it is also a warning for us today. The spirit of Jezebel and the spirit of whoredoms is at work in the world and in the church today.

And it came to pass when Joram saw Jehu that he said, "Is it peace, Jehu?" And he answered, "What peace, so long as the whoredoms of thy mother Jezebel and her witchcrafts are so many?"

2 Kings 9:22, KJV

Freemasonry is the worship of many gods and many idols which is whoredoms. Jezebel is the bride of Freemasonry. We only need to look at our generational line to see if this spirit is at work in other family members. Using our spiritual authority, we can break Jezebel's influence from off of ourselves and off of our family to stop this unfruitful cycle. The following is a prayer of repentance and renunciation.

Prayer to Repent and Renounce Jezebel and Whoredoms

Father, in Jesus' name, I repent for myself and on behalf of my family for operating in a Jezebel spirit. I realize all the attributes and characteristics discussed above and in the Bible about Jezebel is sin and destroys my life and my children's lives and is also offensive to You. Please forgive me and my family for rebelling against You in this way. I cut off from my spirit, soul, and body this ungodly tie and cut this ungodly tie from off of my family through the power of the name of Jesus. I break this ungodly covenant and all vows, oaths, and agreements with Jezebel that I and my family have spoken and acted upon. I declare that the blood of Jesus Christ avail for me and for my family and that our generational lineage is in covenant with You Lord God Almighty, maker of heaven and earth. I renounce all of my agreements spoken in word and by my actions with this spirit of Jezebel and Ashteroth and I apply the blood of Jesus over my life and over the doorposts of my family in the power of the name of Jesus. Father, I ask You to forgive me for harboring any offense and unforgiveness towards any person or any organization. Cleanse my heart and mind from this offense. I give up any obligation on their part to make things right and release these people to You Lord God to bless them. I am Your daughter or son and I trust You Father God to validate who I am in Jesus' name. Lord Jesus, thank You for exposing the work of Jezebel in my life. I acknowledge that I had many if not all of these traits and no longer want to partner with them or give them any room to operate in my life. Please forgive me for thinking and acting this way and aligning with these harmful and hurtful attitudes. I renounce usurping authority, twisting of the truth of God's word, resisting the Holy Spirit's work in my life, for being selfish and self-centered, for manipulating others, for all perversion and deception, and for allowing my heart to be turned away from loving You Lord Jesus, the one who unconditionally loves me. Lord God, cleanse my mind, will, and emotions and renew a right spirit within me that I would walk and live in Your Truth. As I place my trust in You, I receive all Your goodness and grace upon my life. Thank You for setting me free from the influence and control of Jezebel in Jesus' name. Amen.

Take time each day to read scripture to allow your thinking to change and your mind to be transformed. The Holy Spirit will counsel, teach, and comfort us in this new and better way of living.

The Strongman of Religious Spirit

The second stronghold exposed during this City Tour was the religious spirit. Closely related to the religious spirit is Kundalini, Python or divination, and Herod which is a political spirit.

Let's looks at what this second strongman looks like and how it functions. This strongman, the Religious Spirit is comprised of the following.

- Religious Spirit
- Kundalini; Alternate Religious System
- Python/Divination
- Herod/Political Spirit

Religious Spirit

A religious spirit is a demonic principality that has a works mentality requiring us to perform and earn our way to God and to eternal life. A religious spirit has difficulty accepting the work of Jesus at the cross and that it is only through the blood of Jesus that we come into relationship with God and have power to overcome evil in this world. A religious spirit would rather have a set of rules for people to abide by and a set of rituals for them to observe. These rules and rituals can easily be seen in people's lives. By keeping these rules and rituals, a religious spirit can know who is righteous or not. But God's grace and righteousness is of the heart. Grace is known by how we demonstrate love towards one another. Grace does not measure how well we keep rules and whether or not we are maintaining man-made rituals. When we love one another, we will keep the Ten Commandments that God gave to Moses for guidelines as to how we should live.

The Pharisees and Sadducees are examples of those who had a religious spirit in the New Testament and examples for us today. A religious spirit strives to keep the law to the letter and is performance-based, which is the opposite of having an intimate relationship with God, Jesus, and the Holy Spirit. A spirit of religion is in direct opposition to intimate relationship with the Godhead. A religious spirit will deceive people causing them to follow false religious practices that do not honor God or embrace Jesus Christ as Savior. This deception causes people to feel like they must perform well to earn their way to God and to eternal life, when it is a free gift given by grace. It is by grace because someone else paid for it. We cannot earn it or pay for it.

A religious spirit will manifest in different ways to lead people astray. Some people may feel they are not good enough for God to use them, others may have a false holiness and be self-righteous, others may have difficulty believing God is good and has good plans for them. All these beliefs are based in our performance and come from a religious spirit functioning in our lives. Everything God has for us is given by faith through grace. Faith requires relationship.

Some common religious spirits include: judgementalism, self-righteousness, religious pride, criticism, legalism, perfectionism, division, doctrinal falsehood, unbelief, doubt, confusion, argumentum, salvation by works, guilt, condemnation, fear of losing salvation, an unhealthy fear of God, and intolerance with others.[27]

A religious spirit would rather see someone judged and punished for what they did wrong than to see them repent and receive forgiveness from the grace of God. That is because a religious spirit is performance based up-holding to their own man-made laws and rules. That is one of the reasons why the Pharisees and Sadducees became so upset when Jesus healed people. When we try to follow our religious rules and laws it will always interfere with God's forgiveness and grace. God's forgiveness and grace will always cause an upheaval with a religious spirit. A religious spirit will always see themselves as superior to others because they believe they have earned a good standing with God through their works and the other person hasn't.

A religious spirit will criticize others for hanging out with an unsaved person just like they criticized Jesus for going home with a tax collector. A religious spirit criticized the woman who poured expensive perfume over Jesus' feet and washed them with her tears and her hair. They did not understand that act represented Jesus being anointed and prepared for his death on the cross and resurrection. These are heavy burdens a religious spirit lays upon others. Heavy burdens require us to fulfill the law and comply with tradition while omitting more important matters of justice, mercy, and faith.

For they bind heavy burdens, hard to bear, and lay them on men's shoulders, but they themselves will not move them with one of their fingers.
Matthew 23:4, NKJV

Woe to you, scribes and Pharisees, hypocrites! For you pay tithe of mint and anise and cummin, and have neglected the weightier matters of the law: justice and mercy and faith. These you ought to have done, without leaving the others undone.

Matthew 23:23, NKJV

A religious spirit hates the grace of God. It will not allow the Holy Spirit to move in its environment. It is anti-Christ. Therefore, it will not allow the gifts of the Holy Spirit to function in its environment. Neither will a religious spirit manifest the fruit of the Spirit because a religious spirit is not full of God's grace.

Someone who is influenced by a religious spirit will find it difficult to receive new revelation of scripture when it is revealed and to move into a new season that God has prepared for them. When a people are steeped in their religious practices and traditional ways, they miss the leading of the Holy Spirit and the revelation He wants to give to them. That is why a religious spirit persecutes the people who choose to move into the new season that God has for them and follow the new revelation that the Holy Spirit is giving them. That is why there was martyrdom by denominations who maintained religious beliefs and chose not to receive the new revelation or the people moving with this new revelation during the time when God was building and restoring His church.

A religious spirit hides behind its good works because it does not want to be exposed in a person's life or in a region. Occult means to be hidden. A religious spirit borders on the occult. A religious spirit also borders on witchcraft because its prayers are not led or inspired by the Holy Spirit. A religious spirit will allow someone to become born again but will not want them to believe there is anything more such as the baptism of the Holy Spirit and a heavenly prayer language. A religious spirit denies the power of God because it has its own form of godliness, which is to keep the law, do good, meet performance standards to be approved, maintain all the traditional rituals that have been established in a denomination or in a family, and observe all the traditions that go with it.

Having a form of Godliness, but denying its power. Have nothing to do with such people.
2 Timothy 3:5, NIV

A religious spirit invokes guilt and condemnation because the person can never live up to the standards that are required.

My guilt has overwhelmed me, like a burden too heavy to bear.
                                                    Psalms 38:4, NIV

In Andrew Wommack's Charis Bible College Course *Heart Essence of the Gospel* it was noted that 72 percent of those in mental institutions are born again Christians who are laden with guilt and condemnation. They are mentally unstable because they believe they have done something that God is not able to forgive them of. This is guilt and condemnation![28]

Now, the Holy Spirit does convict us of sin so we can be pricked in the heart and turn away from sin. This may produce a guilt feeling in us because we are going in a wrong direction. It is only meant to turn us in a different direction. The Holy Spirit will lead us in a way that frees us of that sin and frees us of any guilt. The Holy Spirit does not ever condemn us.

As in the Days of Midian

As I studied in the Charis Bible College Course the book of Galatians notes that guilt and condemnation are witchcraft. Wommack stated, "If you feel you are not good enough then you are under the law, and it is a curse. If you feel condemnation and guilt; you are being controlled and it causes confusion."[29]

Witchcraft is any controlling and manipulative spirit that tries to put someone under the dominion of someone else. It could be out of a wrong spirit that someone uses scripture in a twisted way to guilt another person into doing a certain thing. That is a religious spirit and is witchcraft. It is operating in control and manipulation. The Holy Spirit operates in grace and convicts us so He can lead us.

The problem Jesus had with the Pharisees was, they took God's truth and turned it into a religious system! They replaced the inner reality of a relationship with God with a system that focused on outward appearances.

Woe to you, [self-righteous] scribes and Pharisees, hypocrites! For you clean the outside of the cup and of the plate, but inside they are full of extortion and robbery and self-indulgence (unrestrained greed). You [spiritually] blind Pharisee, first clean the inside of the cup and of the plate [examine and change your inner self to conform to God's precepts], so that the outside [your public life and deeds] may be clean also.
Matthew 23:25-26, AMP

The Pharisees insisted on following a religious system devoid of the Holy Spirit. They appeared to be righteous but lacked an authentic relationship with the Lord. Their devotion was to the Mosaic Law and not to God. The religious spirit wants to look good, holy, and righteous, but is none of that. Attending church is not God's goal. God looks at the heart of a person.

But if you are led by the Spirit, you are not under the Law.
Galatians 5:18, NIV

The Pharisees knew their theology down to the most minute detail, but when the Son of God Himself walked among them, they did not recognize Him. They were blind to the things for which they claimed to be experts. The religious spirit blames God for everything that happens on earth. Teaching to understand the religious spirit and how it operates will help to expose it in our lives. If we would begin fulfilling our destinies rather than religious obligations the enemy would fear us.[30]

The gift of God is eternal life through Jesus Christ. We cannot earn it, pay for it, study enough for it, or do enough good works to receive it. It is a gift. To as many as receive him, they shall be called the children of God.

For God so loved the world that he gave his one and only Son that whoever believes in him shall not perish but have eternal life.
                                        John 3:16, NIV

If you have never prayed a prayer like this before and if you don't know that you have eternal life, then I invite you to pray this prayer with me. It says He has written these things that we might know that we have eternal life. He wants us to know. We can never be good enough for it, but He gives it to us. All we need to do is receive it.

Salvation Prayer

Dear Lord, I want to thank You, for sending Your son, to die on the cross for me, and for paying my penalty of sin. Lord, I ask You now, to please save me, and deliver me from death. By faith, I receive Your love, and Your salvation, that is freely given, through Jesus Christ, just by asking. So, Lord, I ask You by faith for this wonderful free gift of eternal life and of being called Your child, in Jesus' name. Amen.

Kundalini an Alternate Religious System

In Genesis 3, satan presented to mankind an alternate pathway to what God had offered to Adam and Eve. His pathway would include a counterfeit everlasting life ("You surely will not die.") as well as divine status and enlightenment ("Your eyes will be opened, and you will be like God knowing good and evil.") [31]

"You will not certainly die." the serpent said to the woman. "For God knows that when you eat from it your eyes will be opened, and you will be like God, knowing good and evil."
Genesis 3:4-5, NIV

111

As in the Days of Midian

The alternate religious system that satan established encompasses many different forms (of false religions and philosophies of life) and spans everything that has raised itself up against a true knowledge of God.[32]

We demolish arguments and every pretension that sets itself up against the knowledge of God, and we take captive every thought to make it obedient to Christ.
2 Corinthians 10:5, NIV

Kundalini is a false religion that attracts many because it comes disguised as a pathway that appears to be good. Kundalini originates from the sacred scriptures of Hinduism back from the 5th Century. The word Kundalini is derived from the Sanskrit word *kundal* meaning "coiled energy."[33]

Adam and Eve were offered a pathway that was disguised as good and promised to open their eyes to good and evil but turned out to be a great deception. This caused them to lose the glory God had given them and eventually caused much death and heartache within their family.

Names of false religions are given as such because their name reveals the workings behind that false religion. A coiled energy is not the same Spirit of God that hovered over the earth in Genesis 1 in the beginning. All false religions have one origin, Lucifer (pre-fall from Heaven name) or Satan (post-fall from Heaven name). Satan mimics everything God creates and does. Therefore, satan also has a holy spirit, but it is not the same as the Holy Spirit of God. Kundalini represents a counterfeit holy spirit and is also known as the Queen of Heaven or Lucifera, the feminine side of Lucifer. Satan also mimics the gifts of the true Holy Spirit and desires to deceive many. The Queen of Heaven is known by many other names; Jezebel, Isis, Diana, Mother Earth, Mary, Astarte or Ishtar, Ashtoreth, Kundalini and many others depending on the culture of the people.

> *Many will say to Me on that day, 'Lord, Lord, did we not prophesy in Your name, and in Your name drive out demons, and in Your name perform many miracles?' Then I will tell them plainly, 'I never knew you. Away from me, you evildoers!'*
> Matthew 7:22:23, NIV

Kundalini is in the center of the New Age Movement which is based in occult practice.[34] Like satan in the beginning promised Adam and Eve that if they would partake of what God had warned them not to partake of, they would become enlightened and have a knowing of good and evil, which is a shift in their consciousness. Kundalini teaches the practice of yoga as a way of becoming enlightened and allowing this "coiled energy" that is positioned at the base of one's spine, to open and be released to travel up one's spine. As this energy travels up a person's spine, it claims to affect the seven different chakras of the body which are psychic centers. Because of this occult energy flowing through the spine, it is travels into the nervous system of the body. [35]

The word yoga comes from the Sanskirt root word "yuz." It means to yoke, to unite. It is the yoking together with Hindu gods.[36]

Kundalini forms the foundation of Freemasonry. The 33 degrees of Freemasonry correspond to the 33 vertebrae of the spine through which Kundalini's chi energy rises to the crown chakra at the top of the head, opening the person to the occult Realm of Illumination or Enlightenment and supposed union with Lucifer. This destiny is the ultimate goal of Satan's Alternate Religious System.[37]

Diane Hawkins of Restoration in Christ Ministries at www.rcm-usa.org offers free renunciations for those desiring to repent and renounce their involvement in these types of practices.[38]

Python/Divination

Python is a term that comes from the Greek word *puthon*. The word was derived from the Pythian Oracle at Delphi. For this reason, python is synonymous with divination. A dragon serpent offspring of Gaia who is the goddess Mother Earth. Python was guardian of the oracles (divinatory prophecies) at Delphi. The serpent who was supposedly slain by Apollo to empower him to excel in divinatory prophetics.[39]

A Pythonic Spirit is a spirit of divination manifested by means of inquiring of a familiar spirit. Often this was done through séance' or necromancy.[40]

A python spirit and a religious spirit are much the same. They both seek to silence our voice. Python operates through witchcraft, false prophesy, and divination. The Oracles of Delphi is the place where the Greek prophets (false prophets) spoke from.

As in the Days of Midian

It happened that as we were on our way to the place of prayer, we were met by a slave girl who had a spirit of divination (that is, a demonic spirit claiming to foretell the future and discover hidden knowledge), and she brought her owners a good profit by fortune-telling.

Acts 16:16, AMP

One day, as we were going to the house of prayer, we encountered a young slave girl who had an evil spirit of divination, the spirit of Python. She had earned great profits for her owners by being a fortune-teller.

Acts 16:16, TPT

Here we see python operating through a slave girl who is shouting out to Paul and Silas as they were going to the house of prayer. This girl was shouting a true word, but Paul could discern that something was off about it. It irritated him and he felt manipulated by it in his inner witness. Python is rooted in divination which is an occult practice.

Divination (from Latin *divinare*, *'to foresee, to foretell, to predict, to prophesy'*) is the attempt to gain insight into a question or situation by way of an occultic, standardized process or ritual. Used in various forms throughout history, diviners ascertain their interpretations of how a querent should proceed by reading signs, events, or omens, or through alleged contact or interaction with a supernatural agency.[41]

Python brings confusion, weariness, frustration, and depression. The words it speaks are a counterfeit to the prophetic. When we feel like we have been distracted from our purpose and vision, it may be we have faced resistance from a spirit of python. This is what Paul was discerning as this woman was shouting out to them.

She kept following us, shouting, "These men are servants of the Great High God, and they're telling us how to be saved!"

Acts 16:17, TPT

As Paul and Silas were on their way to the house of prayer, they were sidetracked by this slave girl. The spirit of python seeks to distract our attention and then enslave us. It distracts those on their way to their calling by keeping them out of the secret place of prayer with Father through annoyances, disturbances, and noise. This causes us to lose focus and even our purpose.

The ambitions of python are to wear us down through mockery. It will scorn and mock us individually and cause us to question if the dreams in our hearts are from God or even possible. Just as this slave girl did to Paul and Silas, it will shout at us relentlessly and cause a weariness and confusion. This python, snake-like spirit, constricts and squeezes the life out of its prey. Python seeks to expose, strip, and beat down those serious about fulfilling their call. It accuses those in a public manner with lies and judgments and will try to poison our witness.

A great crowd gathered, and all the people joined in to come against them. The Roman officials ordered that Paul and Silas be stripped of their garments and beaten with rods on their bare backs.

Acts 16:22, TPT

A normal human response when faced with opposition is to run and not face it head on. Paul demonstrates how to turn toward an attack like this, and away from the noise by commanding it to leave in Jesus' name. He didn't speak negatively about the circumstances, but discerned the voice was off, and spoke to it to be silenced.

Day after day she continued to do this, until Paul, greatly annoyed, turned and said to the spirit indwelling her, "I command you in the name of Jesus, the Anointed One, to come out of her now!" At that very moment, the spirit came out of her!

Acts 16:18, TPT

Paul and Silas' presence threatened the income being made through divination and fortune telling so they were beaten and thrown into prison with their hands and feet chained. Instead of giving into despair they chose to praise God anyway in the dark captivity of their discomfort and wounded bodies.

Paul and Silas, undaunted, prayed in the middle of the night and sang songs of praise to God, while all the other prisoners listened to their worship.

Acts 16:24, TPT

Worship is a weapon of warfare and causes angelic assistance to intervene on our behalf. When the assistance of heaven came to rescue Paul and Silas, the ground shook and their chains broke releasing them from prison captivity. Because that region was under the domain of python, the earthquake may have been a supernatural sign of the spirit of python being ripped off that region.

As in the Days of Midian

Suddenly, there was such a violent earthquake that the foundations of the prison were shaken. At once all the prison doors flew open, and everyone's chains came loose.
Acts 16:26, NIV

Not only did Paul and Silas' chains break off while they were in prison, but all of the other prisoners became freed also. The jailer and his entire family gave their hearts to Jesus. Our breakthroughs are not just for us, but they are for others as well.

After they prayed, the place where they were meeting was shaken. And they were all filled with the Holy Spirit and spoke the word of God boldly.
Acts 4:31, NIV

In Acts 28, Paul encounters another snake, but this time it is a physical one. As he was gathering a pile of brushwood for a fire, a venomous snake latched onto his hand. With a shake of Paul's hand, the snake flew into the fire. The people around him were alarmed when the poison from the snake did not kill him.

*When Paul had gathered an armful of brushwood and was
setting it on the fire, a venomous snake was driven out by
the heat and latched onto Paul's hand with its fangs. But
Paul shook the snake off, flung it into the fire, and suffered
no harm at all.*

Acts 28:3,5, TPT

Prayer literally shakes off the attacks from your life
and drops snakes into the fires of God. We only must
decree and speak to the problem, turning our affection
towards Father and command python to leave in the name
of Jesus! As we pray and lift our songs of worship, there
will be a shaking off all that has been opposing us.

*I have given you authority to trample on snakes and
scorpions and to overcome all the power of the enemy;
nothing will harm you.*

Luke 10:19, NIV

Python also hides in the place of the threshold of a
door. A threshold is a place of an open door where we cross
over from one place to the next that God has for us. As we
are positioned to step over the threshold, a python may
attempt to grab a hold of us unaware to stop us. As we step
through an open door, that is a time of change and that is
where python shows up. When we feel weary, sick,

confused, fearful, in doubt, intimidated or in lack, this may be a python spirit with a religious-occultish goal that keeps us from moving forward and being free.

> *No weapon forged against you will prevail, and you will refute every tongue that accuses you.*
> Isaiah 54:17a, NIV

We are in a time when God is opening doors of new beginnings. It is a time of a Third Reformation. As we transition into this new era, we are exhorted to be alert, listen, and pray as we take our steps of faith. God wants to help us unlock our land and territory to be free from a python spirit.

Prayer to Repent and Renounce Python

Heavenly Father, I repent for my involvement with a Python spirit and with divination and with false prophesy. I do not want my voice to be used in this manner, I only want to do that which pleases You and bring glory to You. I repent for allowing any practices of sorcery, dealings with mediums, channeling with spirit guides, using the Ouija board, tarot cards, astrology, Reiki, hypnosis, automatic writing, horoscopes, numerology, the Enneagram, all types of fortune telling, palm readings, New Age spirituality, and

122

anything else associated with the occult or with satan. In the name of Jesus Christ who came in the flesh, and by the power of his Cross, his Precious Blood, and his Resurrection, I renounce and forsake my involvement in all of these, and I choose You alone. Lord Jesus, I confess all these sins before You and ask You to cleanse and forgive me for my divided heart. I renounce the Python spirit, divination, and false prophesy and say that I give it no place for these to work in my life. I ask You Holy Spirit to baptize me afresh with love just as You baptized Your disciples on the day of Pentecost. Thank You Heavenly Father for strengthening my inner spirit with the power of Your Holy Spirit, so that Christ may dwell fully in my heart. In Jesus' name. Amen.

Herod or Political Spirit

I had not ever heard of a Herod spirit until I had that prophetic word in 2011 from Frank Bray telling me to beware of Herod's. That was when I remembered this dream that I had and believed it represented a Herod spirit. It was Herod that rose up to kill the children two years old and younger after Jesus was born. Herod did this because he wanted to kill baby Jesus so Jesus would not grow up to be a king as reported by the wisemen.

Dream April 18, 2008

I was taking care of a toddler. I knew it was a toddler because he was sitting on the floor with a pacifier in his mouth. Standing at the kitchen sink in my basement apartment (in my dream), I looked out the window and saw the legs of a man walking on the sidewalk. He was walking toward the door of my apartment. I knew this man was after my 2-year-old toddler. I was thinking how I could escape with my 2-year-old toddler but realized I didn't have time. Therefore, I hid the 2-year-old toddler in my pantry. I was not sure of how this guy would make entry into my home because he would have to enter against my will.
End of dream.

My Interpretation: The man I saw in my dream walking by my kitchen window, was a person I had gone out with several times but had just stopped. I believe this dream represented a type of evil spirit working through him. I knew he represented a Herod-type of a spirit, because its intention was to kill the toddler I had in the house. The toddler represented those things God had planted inside of me through reading scripture, praying, through desires, dreams, promises, prophetic words, and giftings. This dream was a warning.

Later, I received this prophetic word given by Frank Bray on March 18, 2011. *"There are Herods out there that would want to come along and rob from you. They will try to get in through your windows and doors."*

God gives us prophetic words for edification, exhortation, and comfort. It also helps to write our dreams in a journal to reference later. We will come to see and understand what God is speaking to us and builds our lives upon the wisdom and knowledge that He imparts to us.

But (on the other hand) the one who prophesies speaks to people for edification (to promote their spiritual growth) and (speaks words of) encouragement (to uphold and advise them concerning the matters of God) and (speaks words of) consolation (to compassionately comfort them).
1 Corinthians 14:3, AMP

Because of this dream and prophetic word, I searched out the meaning of the Herod spirit to gain some understanding.

125

As in the Days of Midian

Then He charged them, saying, "Take heed, beware of the leaven of the Pharisees and the leaven of Herod."
Mark 8:15, NKJV

According to the Webster American 1828 Dictionary of the English Language *beware* means: *literally, to restrain or guard one's self from. Hence, to regard with caution, to restrain oneself from anything that may be dangerous, injurious, or improper, to avoid, to take care; followed by of before the thing that is to be avoided. Beware of all, but most beware of man.*[42]

In the above scripture, Jesus was telling the Disciples to be alert and attentive to spiritual challenges they would face from the Pharisees and from Herod.

According to the Webster American 1828 Dictionary of the English Language *leaven* means: *1) a mass of sour dough when mixed with a larger quantity of dough, produces fermentation in it and renders it light. During the seven days of Passover, no leaven was permitted to be in the houses of the Jews Exodus 12. 2) Anything which makes a change in the general mass. It generally means something which corrupts or depraves that with which it is mixed.*[43]

Just as yeast permeates the ingredients that affect bread making, the Pharisees and Herod were creating laws that were overbearing and ungodly, which could permeate the spiritual health of the people of God. The Pharisees were religious leaders and experts in the law who instead of following the Ten Commandments that God gave to Moses, created additional laws that people were required to follow such as a compulsory hand washing ritual including pouring water from a special cup alternately, over their hands exactly four times while chanting a prescribed phrase. This burden, along with hundreds of additional laws could overwhelmingly permeate life and distract people from the teaching of the One True God.[44]

That we should no longer be children, tossed to and fro and carried about with every wind of doctrine, by the trickery of men, in the cunning craftiness of deceitful plotting,
Ephesians 4:14, NKJV

Herod was a king who thought he was god and expected to be treated and honored as such. This may have been challenging for the people at that time because it could have distracted their worship of the one true God and even cause division among the people.

As in the Days of Midian

We see how this played out with King
Nebuchadnezzar who thought he was god and had a golden
image constructed for himself. This image was 90 feet tall
and 9 feet wide and when musical instruments sounded, all
the people were to bow to this statue and worship it.
Shadrach, Meshack, and Abednego chose not to bow down
to this statute or to worship it. They were not distracted by
this leaven. They were thrown into a hot fiery furnace as
the king's warning to everyone else who might also choose
not to comply. But God rescued them.

There is much leaven today in many false
influences and we must not let this leaven dictate, change
or distract us from living out the truth of the Bible. We
must guard our hearts from allowing worldly leaven of
false spiritual teaching, a tainted gospel, or any evil fear to
permeate our lives, but hold fast to the truth of God's Word
and seek to follow His perfect will.

And do not be conformed to this world, but be transformed
by the renewing of your mind, that you may prove
what is that good and acceptable and perfect will of God.
Romans 12:2, NKJV

A Herod spirit makes alliances with the religious
and Jezebel spirits to forward its own hidden agenda. The

political spirit is assigned to block the establishment of the government of the Kingdom of God on the earth by instituting false government and corrupt political practices. It is the spirit behind the positioning and strife in earthy governments and divisions in the Church. The political spirit is the hidden mastermind using the spirit of Islam to spread terrorism and anarchy across the globe.[45]

The Church has become entwined and common with the political system in its operation when it condones its members in the participation of secret societies or when it doesn't offer teachings warning people about them. Accurate and helpful teaching could equip people to be delivered and set free of all those ungodly covenants made by the oaths and vows from these secret societies. When a church does not teach or allow its members to move in the gifts of the Holy Spirit that church becomes more like a worldly kingdom instead of the Kingdom of God. The façade of corrupt governing systems and religious hypocrisy of our day must be exposed so a Herod spirit can no longer cause people to lose their moral compass in the pursuit of power.[46]

As in the Days of Midian

Herod and Jezebel killed John the Baptist. Herod is concerned with what people think and is occupied with reputation and public opinion. When a church does not want to be involved in politics and inform their people what is morally right and wrong in culture, they are working together with a political spirit. It is compromise. Both Daniel in Babylon and Joseph in Egypt had to confront and overcome the strongman of the political spirit to walk in their God-given assignments.

The church is called to be involved in the politics of government. If the church was speaking up on what is right and what is wrong and making a stand for that, we would not have the political confusion today. The church should not have allowed prayer to go out of the schools. The church should not have allowed abortion to go on for 50 years. The church should not have allowed transgender bills to be passed. It is in the political realm that angels and demons fight and where a believer's prayers are effectual. God's army of believers will have wisdom to establish and maintain true government in their lives and in the church providing solutions to the world.

God's government will be established as we align our lives to His divine order, first individually and then corporately. As God establishes true apostolic government, the spirit of Herod in the Church will be exposed.[47]

Prayer to Repent and Renounce a Herod Spirit
I have full jurisdiction in my life, home, family, space of employment, and personal business interests over the schemes of the enemy. The enemy has no legal authority to interfere with what I am working on in my jurisdiction. I put on the full armor of God, I have His Word, and I have God's Spirit to help me guard these areas. I guard my heart from wounds the enemy wants to put on me and walk in humility, love, grace, peace, and authority. This is my identity. I have control over myself and my life and the things concerning me. I do not give that control to anyone else or any evil spirit. I can forgive and love humans, but I war against the spirit using them. I choose who I am in relationship with and to what extent I am in relationship with them. I keep my thoughts and my life pure and in line with God. God Almighty is my Father, and I am His daughter.

As in the Days of Midian

The Strongman of Witchcraft

The third stronghold exposed during this City Tour was witchcraft. Closely related to Witchcraft are Bitterness and Jealousy and Shamanism.

Let's look at what this third strongman looks like and how it functions in each of the following areas.

- Witchcraft
- Bitterness and Jealousy
- Shamanism

Witchcraft

According to Webster's American 1828 Dictionary, *witchcraft* means: *the practices of witches; sorcery; enchantments; intercourse with the devil. Power more than natural.*[48]

Witchcraft was forbidden in Israel.

As in the Days of Midian

*When you enter the land the LORD your God is giving you,
do not learn to imitate the detestable ways of the nations
there. Let no one be found among you who sacrifices their
son or daughter in the fire, who practices divination or
sorcery, interprets omens, engages in witchcraft, or casts
spells, or who is a medium or spiritist or who consults the
dead. Anyone who does these things is detestable to
the LORD; because of these same detestable practices
the LORD your God will drive out those nations before
you. You must be blameless before the LORD your God.*

Deuteronomy 18:9-14, NIV

Witchcraft was introduced to Israel by Jezebel.

*When Joram saw Jehu he asked, "Have you come in peace,
Jehu?" "How can there be peace," Jehu replied, "as long
as all the idolatry and witchcraft of your mother Jezebel
abound?"*

2 Kings 9:22, NIV

Witchcraft was condemned by the Prophets.

*I will destroy your witchcraft and you will no longer cast
spells.*

Micah 5:12, NIV

Witchcraft is the work of the flesh.

134

The acts of the flesh are obvious: sexual immorality, impurity and debauchery; idolatry and witchcraft; hatred, discord, jealousy, fits of rage, selfish ambition, dissensions, factions and envy; drunkenness, orgies, and the like. I warn you, as I did before, that those who live like this will not inherit the kingdom of God.
Galatians 5:19-21, NIV

When our children were very young, I began attending a nearby church so they could attend Sunday school. Shortly after beginning to attend this church, I received an unexpected phone call from one of the leaders. This leader asked me why my husband was not attending church with me. I told him that my husband did not want to come to church. He proceeded to suggest that I encourage him to attend church with me. I explained that I have shared with him my desire for him to come to church with me, but he didn't want to and that I could not force him to come with us. Then this leader continued to suggest to me that I should pay a tithe to the church on my husband's income. I had already given a tithe on my own monthly income, but this leader was suggesting I give a tithe off my husband's income also. I told this leader that I would only give a tithe from my income and that I would not be giving anything from my husband's income.

As in the Days of Midian

All during this phone call I was questioning the purpose of this leader contacting me. First, I thought it was strange that he suggested I attempt to make my husband come to church. It would have been nice if he would have come with us, but he wouldn't so I was going alone with our children. Then I thought this leader was really out-of-line telling me that I should tithe off my husband's income. I knew the principle of tithing and had always done so from my own income.

When this phone call ended, I sat down in a state of wonderment, to ponder on the whole conversation and talk to the Lord about it because it was so unusual. I journaled the aspects of that conversation. This leader did not know or ever meet my husband. He did not ask why my husband was not coming to church, he just told me it was up to me to see that my husband attended church. I wrote in my journal what I discerned spiritually working behind this leader or this church and what I sensed in the natural during this phone call.

I felt the influence of *control*. By insisting that I make my husband attend church and tithe off his income, this pastor was putting a responsibility on me that did not belong on me.

The next influence I discerned was *condemnation.* This leader was a person of authority and did not ask to talk with my husband or make a friendly visit, but instead made me feel that I needed to do what he was strongly asking me to do. Because he was a person of authority, I felt condemnation from him because I was not doing what he was asking me to do. He was misusing his authority.

The other influence I sensed was *confusion.* It seemed strange that this leader was calling me in the middle of the day to talk about my husband and our money. It seemed strange that he was telling me to make sure my husband attend church and that I needed to tithe off his income. None of this made any sense to me. I felt this leader was really misguided in his thinking. I had not ever talked with this leader before this time about myself or about our home. I could easily identify these three aspects of influence *control, condemnation*, and *confusion* during this phone conversation. As I was talking to the Lord about this phone conversation, and identifying *control, condemnation*, and *confusion,* I asked the Lord what spirit was behind this *control, condemnation*, and *confusion* and I heard the Lord say, "Witchcraft."

As in the Days of Midian

Where there is witchcraft, there is control that is abusive, condemnation that is misplaced, and confusion because it is out of order or out of alignment. This church leader should not have been talking with only me about issues involving our marriage relationship. He should have been talking to both husband and wife. Furthermore, it is beneficial to establish a trusting relationship with people when attempting to mentor them. This sounds close to a religious spirit that is legalistic and requires one to live by the rule of law.

I have used what the Lord taught me through this unordinary conversation many times as a simple guideline to identify when a spirit of witchcraft is operating. If there is *control, condemnation*, and *confusion,* I believe there is an influence of witchcraft. This is manipulation; someone wanting to get you to do, what they want you to do, for their own purposes.

Prayer to Repent and Renounce Witchcraft

I repent and renounce of all my involvement with witchcraft and occult, both willingly or in ignorance, known or unknown. I repent and renounce all contact with witchcraft and the occult, by my ancestors to the third and the fourth and to the tenth generation and beyond. I repent and renounce and all power that I have received from all involvement with witchcraft and the occult. I break all agreements, all pacts, all contacts, all contracts, and all deals with satan. They are null and void, powerless, and broken by the power of Jesus' mighty name and by the power of His blood. I repent and renounce all involvement with Ouija Boards, eight balls, séance's, astrology, horoscopes, fortune telling, and ESP. I repent of and renounce involvement with palm readers, tarot cards, all psychic readings, the third eye, levitation, communication with the dead. I repent and renounce all forms of deception, control, manipulation, and rebellion. I repent and renounce all black magic, all white magic, yoga, meditations, crystals, fetishes, and automatic handwriting. I break all chants, all spells, all vows, all covenants, all incantations, including the effects of Freemasonry. I renounce all sacrifices, blood sacrifices, animal or human, all blood oaths, and all blood vows. I repent and renounce out of body experiences, astral-projection, spirit guides, animal guides, channeling, imaging, tea leaves, pendulum, Indian rites, Indian rituals, all satanic rites, satanic rituals and ceremonies, all witch doctors, sorcery, Santeria, divination, wizardry, voodoo, and reincarnation. I renounce and I repent of all involvement with witchcraft, Wicca, and New Age. I break every hex, every vex, every

*voodoo, all witchcraft. I break every incantation, every
blood oath, blood vow, and blood covenant. I break the
effects of every curse spoken or unspoken over my life from
my mother's side and my father's side back to the third and
the fourth to the tenth generation and beyond. I repent of
and renounce all the effects of all doctrines of demons, all
witchcraft and the occult in Jesus' mighty name and
declare that I am free from all forms of witchcraft in me
and in my home in the power of Jesus' name. Amen.*

Bitterness and Jealousy

Bitterness is a landing strip for witchcraft activity.
Bitter judgment that we have toward others can cause us to
have self-exaltation. God wants to help us examine
ourselves and pull up any bitterroots of judgement because
they will define us.

*Pursue peace with all people and holiness without which
no one will see the Lord. Looking carefully lest anyone fall
short of the grace of God, lest any root of bitterness
springing up causes trouble and by this many become
defiled.*
Hebrews 12:14-15, NKJV

We should pursue peace with all people and all
holiness without which no one will see the Lord: looking
carefully lest anyone should fall short of the grace of God.

Lest any root of bitterness springing up causes trouble by it and many become defiled. This can happen so easily in churches or in families. If we have a bitterness toward someone in our family, it will defile many in our family. This isn't just about us, but it will divide family. The same in ministry if someone has a bitter judgment in their heart and they share it with others, it just poisons everyone and suddenly we feel the atmosphere is no longer impregnated with goodness. It is impregnated with division and witchcraft. Let all bitterness and wrath and anger be put away from us because these do not bring about justice or achieve the righteousness of God. We must watch over our heart with all diligence.

Let all bitterness and wrath and anger and clamour
(perpetual animosity, resentment, strife, fault-finding) and
slander be put away from you, along with every kind of
malice (all spitefulness, verbal abuse, malevolence).
Ephesians 4:31, AMP

When we give ourselves over to bitterness, wrath, anger, evil speaking and malice, we open a door for witchcraft to control us and to work through us and we become a curse rather than a blessing to others. God wants us to be cleansed from that because we need to have unity, love and blessings. We cannot have bitterness in our hearts and expect the Holy Spirit to fill us up.

> *But if you have bitter envy and self-seeking in your hearts do not boast and lie against the truth.*
>
> James 3:14, NKJV

A bitter edge and jealousy will damage our perception and outlook on life. It will also ignite witchcraft in our life opening us up to control and manipulation of others.

> *Judge not that you be not judged. For with what judgement you judge, you will be judged; and with the measure you use it will be measured back to you.*
>
> Matthew 7:1-2, NKJV

When we have a critical judgement against others, it is because we are bitter. It leaves a landing strip for that same thing to come back to us because that was a measure we gave out.

Give, and it will be given to you. They will pour into your lap a good measure—pressed down, shaken together, and running over [with no space left for more]. For with the standard of measurement you use [when you do good to others], it will be measured to you in return.

Luke 6:38, AMP

We become the enemy of God by walking in these contrary things. The cross is the solution to get bitterness and witchcraft out of our heart.

Then Moses led Israel from the Red Sea and they went into the Desert of Shur. For three days they traveled in the desert without finding water. When they came to Marah, they could not drink its water because it was bitter. (That is why the place is called Marah) So the people grumbled against Moses, saying, "What are we to drink?" Then Moses cried out to the LORD, and the LORD showed him a piece of wood. He threw it into the water, and the water became fit to drink.

Exodus 15:22-25, NIV

The people became bitter as they complained and murmured and came against authority. When Moses cried out to the Lord and the Lord showed him a tree. Moses cast the tree into the waters and the waters became sweet. The tree represented the cross that Jesus died on. We also, must pick up the cross and die to ourselves and forgive everyone

143

who hurt us. When we do, our water becomes sweet too. It is the sweet nature of Jesus Christ.

Bitterness can be passed down to our children and to our children's children by our words and attitudes and dislike toward others. Ask Holy Spirit to search your heart to see if there is any bitterness. All we owe people is to love them and desire good for them. Bitterness will destroy our lives and harm those who come after us.

Prayer to Repent and Renounce Bitterness

Father I was treated unfairly and sometimes harshly. The things that happened to me were not right. I don't even know what caused people around me to respond toward me in anger, hatred, and revenge, but Father I do know there is an enemy called satan who wants to stop me from fulfilling my purpose in life and wants to stop me from obtaining the inheritance that You promised for me to have. Father, I choose to forgive them and release them to You. I willingly repent of any bitterness in my heart. Please remove any deception that is clouding my mind. I renounce bitterness and witchcraft that came into me with the bitterness and I command it all to leave me now in the power of the name of Jesus. Holy Spirit go deep into my heart and pull out all bitter roots that planted themselves in me. As I renew my mind with scripture, I will become sweeter every day. Thank You Father, that You have good plans for my life and a happy future. Father I ask that You put Your arms around me and hold me close. I trust You to completely take care of me. In Jesus name I pray. Amen.

Shamanism

Shamanism is a religious practice that is historically associated with indigenous and tribal societies but is practiced by Western people also as a type of New Age spirituality.

Shamanism involves the belief that shamans, with a connection to the otherworld, have the power to heal the sick, communicate with spirits, and escort souls of the dead to the afterlife. People engaged in a form of shamanistic practice may also be known as seers, medicine men, witch doctors, or even witches.

Everything that God has created and loves, satan will mimic and pervert because of his hatred toward God and mankind. Everything that God gives to his creation including human beings, satan will also mimic and pervert for the purpose of defiling human beings. God has provided one way of salvation and eternal life, that is through Jesus Christ the only one who has died on the Cross of Calvary, went to Hell taking back all power and authority from satan and was resurrected out of Hell and death and is now seated at the right hand of God Almighty in Heaven to rule and reign forever. Satan mimics this by offering many ways to eternal life, but these are all counterfeits. When Jesus died and rose again, leaving the earth, the Holy Spirit came to be on earth with mankind to council, comfort, and lead us.

Satan has many evil counterfeits to the Holy Spirit of God. Satan's counterfeits do not bring life or joy, but death and sadness. The Holy Spirit distributes gifts for the equipping of the believers in Christ to assist them in overcoming the things in the world. Satan offers gifts also in counterfeit of the ones the Holy Spirit has for us. Satan's gifts work through witchcraft, divination, and occult and may appear to heal the sick, communicate with spirits, have a power to move objects including human bodies through space and many other things. Satan will always counterfeit who God is and what God does. This is why we are identifying these strongmen and how they function, so we can recognize them and how they differ from the true workings of God, Jesus, and the Holy Spirit.

According to The Prophet's Dictionary by Paula A. Price, Ph.D., *Shamanism* is *"An ancient nature religion of largely indigenous peoples that relies on the spiritual positioning and conditioning of the witch doctor, or tribal priest, in relation to spirit world. Through self or spirit induced trances, the shaman travels between all the worlds, intercepts, and guides departed souls to their right destination, and wrestles for the healing and deliverances of tribal members. The shaman exercises enormous spiritual authority over the tribe and enjoys considerable supernatural powers as well. The crux of the shaman's abilities lies in drug addiction. To operate in the invisible realms of the spirit the shaman must do so with the aid of hallucinogenic drugs to open up to the guide and traverse the spirit realm with their assistance.*"[49]

I heard Martha Lucia speak in Rugby, North Dakota in 2002. She shared a message about the Illuminati, which is the highest level of Freemasonry and is not a very uplifting subject. During this session Martha shared with us that she had seen in the spirit a vision of five Shamans standing across the Northern Tier of the United States; over Idaho, Montana, North Dakota, and Minnesota. Martha stated that these five Shamans represented five strongholds over this Northern Region.[50]

As in the Days of Midian

Martha Lucia did not identify the exact spiritual names of these five Shamans when she shared what she had seen. She may have received that revelation from God later, but I did not hear that from her or hear what those names were.

The Lord was revealing to the people through this Prophet-Watchman that there were five Shaman strongholds over that region. When Bishop Hamon and his team went to Fargo, North Dakota for this City Tour they discerned and identified three strongholds in our region as: Freemasonry, Religion, and Witchcraft. I believe these were three of the five strongholds that Martha Lucia saw as Shamans standing across the Northern Tier of the United States.

During morning prayer with Christian International, I began to ask the Lord about the five Shamans that Martha Lucia saw and was impressed by the Lord they were: Freemasonry, Religion, Witchcraft, Jezebel and Leviathan. These are all closely related in characteristics and how they function in defiling a land and in defiling the people. Having heard this, I studied these strongholds that I believed God had been revealing to the body of Christ in this area for a long time.

Prayer to Repent and Renounce Shamanism

Heavenly Father, I repent and renounce practicing divination, sorcery, interpreting omens, engaging in this type of witchcraft, consulting the dead, having been a traveler/explorer of the spirit world, the belief that we must heal and honor our mother the Earth (who is viewed as a living, conscious organism). I repent and renounce the belief that this sacred female Goddess, the earth must be nourished with our prayers and ceremonies. I repent and renounce for the belief that You Lord God sent Shamans to help humans through sickness, death and hardship. I renounce the shamanic roots found in Hinduism, Buddhism, Taoism, Wicca and Red Indian Magic. I renounce my spirit vision and Strong Eye and the threefold shamanic role of healer, intermediary and psychopomp. I renounce shamanic healing and medicine people (note, Shamans are healers who travel in the spirit realm as well, ordinary medicine men do not). I renounce all shamanic tools used to induce trance, those used to journey and those used to heal. I renounce mastery over fire and fire walking, smudging (cleansing through smoke), centering (focusing energy for power), trancing and journeying as well as all and every other shamanic ceremony and shamanic tool. I renounce all shamanic ceremonies such as pipe smoking, Sweat Lodge Ceremonies, Shamanic Dance and Movement,

As in the Days of Midian

Trance Dancing, dancing the animal, soul retrieval, ceremonies for the dead soul and the vision quest. I renounce the shamanic medicine wheel and its connection to the four elements (water, fire, air and earth) as well as its connection to the spirits of the four directions (north, south, east and west) as well as up and down. I renounce the symbolism in the points of the medicine wheel (grounding, change, passion, power and healing and the center or spirit). I renounce all correspondences used in Shamanism, as well as their properties. I renounce the use of nature, such as herbs, plants, flowers and trees; gemstones, crystals and minerals; and animal feathers in shamanic practice. I repent for having entered the spirit world through a vision or trance, whether induced by spiritual teachers, esoteric practices, drumming, singing, chanting, rattling, dancing or breathing techniques. I renounce the drum and the steady, rhythmic beat of the drum used to enter a shamanic trance. I renounce the dance cycles set to phases of the moon and months of the year. I renounce all hallucinogens, sacred plants or psychedelic drugs (especially magic mushrooms and/or DMT) used to induce a trance or vision. I renounce all magical substances inserted into the body by spirits to enhance shamanic powers. I renounce ALL and EVERY form of shamanic trancing, astral projection and shape shifting (changing into an animal or a bird). I renounce the

seven planes of consciousness in trancing and journeying
(the seven Chakras or psychic centers on the body). I
renounce all traditional animal costumes, headdresses and
bodily painting used in dance to transform spiritually into
an animal. I renounce all shamanic spirits or spirit helpers
that are a part of Shamanism. I renounce the wearing of
masks, skins and claws during ceremonies as well as
imitating the movements, growls and calls of the animal. I
renounce using sacred plants, dancing and drumming to
enter into an altered state of consciousness so as to travel
to the spirit world in the form of the power animal. I
renounce the ancient spirits or spirit guides (the
embodiment of the ancient peoples of the earth). in any way
or form. I repent for and renounce any involvement on my
behalf and for my ancestor's involvement with Shamanism
and occult practices of Shamanism.

Heavenly Father, I ask that you send your angels to escort
these spirits and demons to the place You have reserved for
them until the time of judgment. I declare that all cords,
bonds and ties between myself, and all Shamanistic
practices, are cut and sealed by the Blood of Jesus Christ
of Nazareth. I thank You, Lord, that I, by Your Grace, am
set free from all bondage. I thank you Father that the
bondage of Shamanism in my life is broken. I declare this

As in the Days of Midian

petition sealed with the Blood, Power, and Authority of Jesus Christ. In the Name of Jesus,

Become a Warrior

Army of the Lord Movement

We established earlier in reviewing church history, that we are in a time of the Army of the Lord. If we are truly in the Army of the Lord Movement, then God has more battles ahead that we will need to participate in. These are spiritual battles fought in prayer using spiritual weapons.

Before going to war, we must know who our enemy is and have a strategy of how to overtake him. Victory must be won in prayer in the spirit realm before it can be won in the natural realm. The Army of the Lord Movement is a spiritual movement in prayer led by the Holy Spirit along with the assistance of God's angel army. This is a time for spiritual warriors to take their positions and function in their God-given sphere and purpose. There has always been spiritual warriors or Christians who know how to pray to overcome satan and his demonic horde. This is a time in church history that the Army of the Lord is at the front lines.

153

As in the Days of Midian

The Old Testament and New Testament give many examples for us to gain knowledge and wisdom about who our enemies are. Our enemies are spiritual beings and not the flesh of man. Although, spiritual demonic beings do function through real people, our prayers and decrees are for the purpose of removing and overcoming those spiritual enemies while manifesting the Kingdom of God on earth like Jesus did.

In the natural, there is no freedom without having to fight for it. It is the same in the spiritual. There is a battle occurring in the spiritual realm today that believers in Christ must engage in. The weapons we use to fight in the spiritual realm are not the same weapons as in the natural realm.

For our struggle is not against flesh and blood [contending only with physical opponents], but against the rulers, against the powers, against the world forces of this [present] darkness, against the spiritual forces of wickedness in the heavenly (supernatural) places.
Ephesians 6:12, AMP

Spiritual Weapons

The Name of Jesus

The name of Jesus is a spiritual weapon. Jesus overcame satan and all the powers of hell when He shed His blood on the Cross for the sins of all mankind. The power of God raised Jesus from the dead and sat Him at God's right hand to rule and reign over the earth. Jesus gave those who believed in Him the same authority He had to cast out demons and heal the sick and overcome all the power of the enemy. It is through the power of Jesus' name that gives us the legal right to declare and decree God's will in the earth.

That at the name of Jesus every knee should bow, in heaven and on earth and under the earth.
Philippians 2:10, NIV

The Blood of Jesus

The blood of Jesus is a spiritual weapon. Sin can only be remitted through blood. This was the sacrificial system God put into place when Adam and Eve sinned in the beginning and God had to kill an animal to make a covering for Adam and Eve because they no longer had

God's glory to cover them. Later Moses was instructed to kill a bull or lamb using the blood of an animal at certain times of the year to cover the sins of the people. In the New Testament that was done away with because Jesus became the one-time sacrificial lamb for the whole world by the shedding of His blood. Through the blood of Jesus, we are saved, healed, delivered of demonic influence, and overcome every power, principality, and wickedness in heavenly places.

> *In Him we have redemption through His blood, the forgiveness of sins, according to the riches of His grace.*
> Ephesians 1:7, NKJV

God's Audible Voice

Hearing God's audible voice is a spiritual weapon. God speaks to us with instructions, encouragement, guidance, warnings, and tenderly love. Hearing our Father's voice imparts identity into us and we can know who we are and what His purposes are for us. It helps us to stand in faith and trust in the Lord our God with all of our heart. This encourages us and enables us to stand and speak against unrighteousness and injustice.

Become a Warrior

My sheep hear my voice, and I know them, and they follow me.
John 10:27, NKJV

God Speaking through Dreams and Visions

Hearing God's voice through dreams and visions we have is a spiritual weapon. When we have dreams (night visuals) and visions (day visuals) we many times will experience strong emotions and feelings. God speaks deep into our hearts with these emotions and feelings. Many times, they are how He feels and He is letting us experience His heart on the matter that we are dreaming about. There are many examples in the Bible where God gave people dreams to go certain places or not to go certain places and it saved their lives. Strategies for war were given to men and women in the Old and New Testaments and we can expect to receive this same help from the Lord through dreams and visions He gives to us.

As for these four young men, God gave them knowledge and skill in all literature and wisdom, and Daniel had understanding in all visions and dreams.
Daniel 1:17, NKJV

157

As in the Days of Midian

Our Inner Witness

Hearing God speak to our inner witness is a spiritual weapon. Many times, when we have a thought or hear our conscience speak within us, it is not from us, but from God. God's voice speaking in our inner witness sounds like our own voice, but we can know it is God speaking because it will be something that we did not know in ourselves. When God speaks to our inner witness, it is generally a still small voice that speaks softly and gently to us.

> *Then He said, "Go out, and stand on the mountain before the LORD." And behold, the LORD passed by, and a great and strong wind tore into the mountains and broke the rocks in pieces before the Lord, but the Lord was not in the wind; and after the wind an earthquake, but the LORD was not in the earthquake; and after the earthquake a fire, but the LORD was not in the fire; and after the fire a still small voice.*
> 1 Kings 19:11-13, NKJV

Worship

Singing songs to the Lord in worship is a spiritual weapon. When we worship and praise God, we exalt Him instead of our difficulties and we seek our deliverance or a way through our trials by His ability and not by our own desires or fleshly ways. Singing to the Lord destroys the devil's hold on the spiritual atmosphere around us. It brings joy into our hearts that gives us strength and causes us to look to God and not on our circumstances.

> *But at midnight Paul and Silas were praying and singing hymns to God, and the prisoners were listening to them. Suddenly there was a great earthquake, so that the foundations of the prison were shaken; and immediately all the doors were opened and everyone's chains were loosed.*
> Acts 16:25-26, NKJV

Dance

Dance is a spiritual weapon. David danced before the Lord with all of his might. He even desired to become more undignified in his dance and worship to the Lord, meaning exalting the Lord. Dance is a form of worship to the Lord using our whole body. Our gestures and movements are a prophetic language of adoration to the Lord. It reveals joy when we move our body with grace before the Lord using sounds on musical instruments that exalt Him. Satan was the worship leader in Heaven before he became prideful and was removed from Heaven. Worship was then given to mankind to express in the earth.

As in the Days of Midian

Song and dance and music brings glory to the Lord God
and silences any enemy that would attempt to come near
us.

*Then David danced before the LORD with all his might; and
David was wearing a linen ephod.*
2 Samuel 6:14, NIV

*Now as the ark of the LORD came into the City of
David, Michal, Saul's daughter, looked through a window
and saw King David leaping and whirling before the LORD;
and she despised him in her heart.*
2 Samuel 14:16, NKJV

Shout

The shout is a spiritual weapon. There are many
times in the Bible that God instructed his people to shout to
bring about a victory. In the last day when Jesus returns, it
says he will return with a shout! The word praise in Psalm
145:4 is the Hebrew word *shabach* meaning *to address in a
loud tone, to triumph, to shout, to still, to command, to
glory.* This is shouting praise and stills the enemy,
commanding our victory. Just like a shout caused the walls
of Jericho to fall, our shout causes evil to be dispelled from
our environment also.

One generation shall praise thy works to another and shall declare thy mighty acts.

Psalm 145:4, KJV

Angels

God sends angels to intervene on our behalf. These are a spiritual weapon. Michael, one of the chief angels of heaven assisted Daniel when he prayed. Hebrews 1:14, NIV, "Are not all angels ministering spirits sent to serve those who will inherit salvation?"

Jehovah Sabaoth is one of God's names and it means He is the Lord of Hosts. Sabaoth is a military term meaning a group of fighting men or an army. This army is a heavenly host army and not a natural army on earth. This heavenly army is available to assist us as we make decrees and declarations according to the Word of God, they are sent on assignment to carry them out.

Are not all the angels ministering spirits sent out [by God] to serve (accompany, protect) those who will inherit salvation? [Of course they are!]
Hebrews 1:14, AMP

161

As in the Days of Midian

Gifts of the Holy Spirit

The gifts of the Holy Spirit are spiritual weapons. Gifts of the Holy Spirit are not for the holder, but they are gifts to help others and to bless others with. Gifts of the Holy Spirit will reveal things to us that we did not know in ourselves, they will heal our bodies, they will perform miracles of all kinds depending on what the need is at the moment, they supply us with supernatural faith and power to do exploits in the earth to assist us in overcoming our enemies and bringing aid to believers in Christ and to those who don't know Him.

> *We have different gifts, according to the grace given to each of us. If your gift is prophesying, then prophesy in accordance with your faith; if it is serving, then serve; if it is teaching, then teach; if it is to encourage, then give encouragement; if it is giving, then give generously; if it is to lead do it diligently; if it is to show mercy, do it cheerfully.*
> Romans 12:6-8, NIV

Prayer

Prayer is a spiritual weapon. Prayer is communing with God. It is done mostly in our private lives. Prayer is having relationship with God and sharing our heart with Him and then letting Him share His heart with us. Having a

162

personal relationship with God is powerful when facing off any demon that would try to come against us or bring harm to us.

> *Praying always with all prayer and supplication in th Spirit, being watchful to the end with all perseverance and supplication for all the saints.*
> Ephesians 6:18, NKJV

Praying in the Spirit

Praying in the Spirit with your heavenly language is a powerful spiritual weapon. Satan nor any of his demons understand what we are speaking to God when we pray in our heavenly language. Only our spirit inside of us and the spirit of God knows what is being spoken. If we listen to our inner witness or our spirit inside of us, we can hear or have a sense of knowing some of what that conversation is with God. Praying in our spirit language builds up our inner man. Jude 1:20, NIV, "But you, dear friends, by building yourselves up in your most holy faith and praying in the Holy Spirit." It is possible to be always praying by praying by using our heavenly spiritual language. We can pray out loud or we can pray quietly, or we can pray within ourselves without using our mouth.

As in the Days of Midian

But you shall receive power when the Holy Spirit has come upon you; and you shall be witnesses to Me in Jerusalem, and in all Judea and Samaria, and to the end of the earth.

Acts 1:8, NKJV

Fasting

Fasting is a spiritual weapon. Fasting can involve food or anything that we take pleasure in. It can be for any length of time and for any purpose. Usually, fasting involves seeking God for direction or answers, for help for another person being healed or delivered in some form, to break strongholds in our lives or city, or for anything that we desire God to help us with. Fasting is a form of dying to ourselves and seeking God's will in a matter.

Is this not the fast that I have chosen: To lose the bonds of wickedness. To undo the heavy burdens. To let the oppressed, go free. And that you break every yoke?"

Isaiah 58:6, NKJV

Speaking God's Word

Speaking the Word or Scriptures in decrees and declarations is a spiritual weapon. When we decree a thing according to God's Word, He says it will be done for us. Jesus spoke words of healing and restoration to people, and it was done for them. That is because He spoke only what He heard the Father speak and did only what He saw the Father do. This is available to us as we walk in relationship with the Lord.

You will also declare a thing, And it will be established for you; So light will shine on your ways.
Job 22:28, NKJV

Prayer of Agreement

The prayer of agreement is a spiritual weapon. Matthew 18:19, NIV says, "Again, truly I tell you that if two of you on earth agree about anything they ask for, it will be done for them by my Father in heaven." The power of agreement as we ask according to the Word of God. No evil enemy can stand before us when we use the Word of God against him in the power of agreement.

Again I say to you that if two of you agree on earth concerning anything that they ask, it will be done for them by My Father in heaven.
Matthew 18:19, NKJV

As in the Days of Midian

Prophetic Words

Prophetic words are a spiritual weapon. The gift of prophecy and prophetic words spoken by those in the office of a prophet are given to strengthen, encourage, comfort, and to also give direction, warnings, and knowledge in how to overcome. Prophetic words do not come about on their own. Prophetic words are God speaking to us and should be treated as very valuable, therefore, written down and read over and meditated upon often. We are to use our prophetic words as a weapon of war.

Timothy, my son, I am giving you this command in keeping with the prophecies once made about you, so that by recalling them you may fight the battle well,
1 Timothy 1:18, NIV

Walking in Love

Walking in love toward others is a spiritual weapon. Love never fails. Many times, situations do not turn out like we hope that they would, but it is possible that our perception or understanding may have been incorrect. Some way and somehow as we carry God's heart of love and compassion, what we set our hands to will not fail and

166

those things we hope for will be seen. Love always overcomes.

Greater love has no one than this: to lay down one's life for
one's friends.
John 15:13, NIV

Living in God's Ways

Governing our lives according to God's ways is a spiritual weapon. As we mature in age and in the Lord through reading scripture and through relationship with the Lord, we learn how to govern our lives in a way that will provide protection for us and give each of us a sound mind. When our godly walls and gates are secure and functioning well, no enemy of darkness can prevail over us. Fear cannot have any power over us and we walk in an overcoming faith.

For God has not given us a spirit of fear, but of power and
of love and of a sound mind.
2 Timothy 1:7, NKJV

Submitting to God

Submitting to God is a spiritual weapon. James 4:7, NIV, "Submit yourselves, then, to God. Resist the devil, and he will flee from you." The devil will flee from us, which includes all of our enemies in the spiritual realm and the natural realm. God says He will fight for us. We are under His wings and under His covering. Our part is to submit to God's authority and to actively resist the devil in prayer and in our daily walk throughout our life.

> *Therefore, submit to God. Resist the devil and he will flee from you.*
>
> James 4:7, NKJV

Honoring Fathers and Mothers

Honoring our fathers and mothers is a spiritual weapon. This is the first command that has a blessing attached to it. If we do not honor our parents, we risk dying prematurely. Even if our parents were not good parents and were abusive toward us, we can give them honor. That doesn't mean what they did was okay or that we even have to be around them if they are still living. Honoring is forgiving and recognizing we have life today because of them and anything that was not good while we were with them, we can now be changed for the better through forgiveness and honoring them.

Honor your father and your mother, so that you may live long in the land the LORD your God is giving you.
Exodus 20:12, NIV

Intercession

Intercession is a spiritual weapon. Intercession is standing in the gap for someone, or our coming before the Lord on behalf of another person to repent for them and ask God to intervene in their lives to help them. Intercession is praying in tongues and praying the Word of God to change the circumstances or situation for a person, or a city, or a region. Abraham did this when God told Abraham he was going to destroy Sodom and Gomorrah. Abraham asked God if he would not destroy these cities if there were 50 righteous people and God says he won't. Then Abraham keeps lowering the number of righteous people until he comes down to 10 and God says he won't destroy these cities if there are 10 righteous people. It turns out there weren't even 10 righteous and these cities were destroyed. God tells us to come boldly before the throne of grace and plead our matter before Him. This is intercession.

As in the Days of Midian

If My people who are called by My name will humble themselves, and pray and seek My face, and turn from their wicked ways, then I will hear from heaven, and will forgive their sin and heal their land.
2 Chronicles 7:14, NKJV

Breaking Ungodly Covenants

Breaking ungodly covenants with idols through vows, oaths, and agreements is a powerful spiritual weapon. When we or our ancestors make vows, oaths, and agreements in secret societies or with people who are involved in these organizations, an ungodly covenant is made and we give satan and all the demons connected to these idol gods and principalities an open-door access to us. It is not until we break those ungodly covenants specifically and not just in a generic prayer, using the blood of Jesus Christ is their influence over us broken off.

When you come into the land which the LORD your God is giving you, you shall not learn to follow the abominations of those nations.
Deuteronomy 18:9, NKJV

Communion

Partaking of communion is a spiritual weapon. When we take communion of the bread and wine we are remembering and proclaiming the death and resurrection of Jesus Christ and all that was wrought in and through that. We are proclaiming that Jesus Christ is Lord of our lives. We take this time to search our hearts and repent if we feel there is a conviction from the Holy Spirit. It is a time of cleansing our motives and attitude and receiving healing, deliverance, and having all our needs met through Christ. This partaking of communion reminds the devil and all his cohorts where we stand and what our position is. It causes wicked spirits in heavenly places and powers and principalities to tremble and shake and lose their influence in our life and region as this is done in a corporate setting.

And when He had given thanks, He broke it and said, Take, eat; this is My body which is broken for you; do this in remembrance of Me. In the same manner He also took the cup after supper, saying, This cup is the new covenant in My blood. This do, as often as you drink it, in remembrance of Me. For as often as you eat this bread and drink this cup, you proclaim the Lord's death till He comes
1 Corinthians 11:24-26, NKJV

God has provided an almost endless number of spiritual warfare weapons. He will speak to us and lead us and tell us what to do and what to say in specific situations. These

171

directives He gives to us are warfare. They are out of the ordinary in the natural realm but are powerful when acted upon in faith in the spiritual realm.

Notice the easy manner that God obtained victory for Gideon in conquest of the Midianites and all the other *ites* that were with them. Beside showing up for the battle, the prophetic acts of; blowing of trumpets; breaking of glass jars, shining lights and shouting was all these 300 warriors did. The voice of the Lord shatters our enemy and the voice of the Lord put to music shatters our enemy. The voice of the Lord was in the breaking of the glass jars and in the blowing of the trumpets, and in the shing of the lights, and in the shouts of the 300 warriors.

The voice of the Lord will shatter Assyria (the enemy) with his rod he will strike them down. Every stroke the Lord lays on them with his punishing club will be to the music of timbrels and harps as he fights them in battle with the blows of his arm.
Isaiah 30:31, NIV

A warrior filled with wisdom ascends into the high place and releases regional breakthrough, bringing down the strongholds of the mighty.
Proverbs 21:22, TPT

Applying these weapons to our lives will dismantle satan's tactics and plans that he sets against us, our families, cities, and our nation.

God is raising up a remnant army of Esther's and Gideon's in every city, region, and nation to stand in the gap on behalf of a people and to do intercession and spiritual warfare. He is purifying His church as He corrects, leads, and instructs. Be encouraged that the Lord has been exposing the darkness in all of our lives, and not just in high places of government. But it is up to us to choose to repent, and renounce when the Holy Spirit corrects us, and turn our hearts towards Him.

The Lord God has been gathering His warriors together in small groups of two or three and in larger settings to be an apostolic hub, an apostolic center where He can send His army angels on strategic missions to accomplish assignments in the spiritual realm bringing the Kingdom of God into the natural realm.

This is a time for the Army of the Lord to pursue, overtake, and recover all.

As in the Days of Midian

Prayer

Father, we thank You for raising up Esther's and Gideon's all over the world to stand in the gap for their families, region and for their nation and wage an effective warfare. We thank You for teachings us how to be warriors and how to use the weapons that You provided for us so that we can be effective overcomers. We pray that the darkness around us would continue to be exposed as we shine our lights of Your glory within each one of us so that Your Kingdom would come and Your will would be done on earth as it is in heaven. Thank You Lord Sabaoth for the Gideon's army that You are raising up to be obedient courageous warriors of faith, that You Lord God are with us and will do valiantly. We give You Lord God all the praise and all the glory! Amen and Hallelujah!

Endnotes

1. www.christianinternationalvisionchurch.org Bishop Bill Hamon, Christian International Ministries, Santa Rosa Beach, Florida

2. Ibid

3. *Webster's American 1828 Dictionary of the English Language* copyright 2010 by The Editorium LLC, West Valley City, UT 84128-3917, Walking Lion Press

4. www.christianinternationalvisionchurch.org Word of the Lord 2023 by Prophet Bill Lackie, Christian International Ministries, Santa Rosa Beach, Florida

5. https://aslansplace.com/language/en/author/paulcox15588/, Aslan's Place, Paul L. Cox

6. www.christianinternationalvisionchurch.org Bishop Bill Hamon, Christian International Ministries, Santa Rosa Beach, Florida

7. Freemasonry; Unlocking Their Secrets DVD/MP4 https://www.ramministry.org/ Sylvie Sudduth

8. Ibid

9. Ibid

10. Ibid

11. Ibid

12. Ibid

13. Ibid

14. Ibid

15. Ibid

16. Ibid

17. Ibid

18. https://marthalucia.com; Martha Lucia Prophet Watchman Christian International Ministries, Santa Rosa Beach, Florida 32459

19. *Freemasonry Death in the Family* copyright 2009 by Yvonne Kitchen ISBN: 0-646-34807-8 Fruitful Vine Publishing House 500 Kelletts Road Lysterfield Victoria 3156 Australia

20. *Power and Prayers to Neutralize Leviathan* copyright 2010 (The I found It! Series) by Joshua Tayo Obi-Gbesan ISBN: 9781609576493 www.zulonpress.com

21. *A to Z Dream Symbology Dictionary* by Dr. Barbie L Breathitt, DreamsDecoder.com, Copyright 2015 ISBN-13: 978-1-942551-02-7 Barbie Breathitt Enterprises, Inc.

22. *Webster's American 1828 Dictionary of the English Language* copyright 2010 by The Editorium LLC, West Valley City, UT 84128-3917, Walking Lion Press

23. *Freemasonry Death in the Family* copyright 2009 by Yvonne Kitchen ISBN: 0-646-34807-8 Fruitful Vine Publishing House 500 Kelletts Road Lysterfield Victoria 3156 Australia

24. https://www.aconsciousrethink.com/13929/signs-playing-mind-games/

25. *Webster's American 1828 Dictionary of the English Language* copyright 2010 by The Editorium LLC, West Valley City, UT 84128-3917, Walking Lion Press

26. Ibid

27. https://www.greatbiblestudy.com/deliverance-ministry/religious-spirits/

28. www.charisbiblecollege.com Heart Essence of the Gospel, Charis Bible College by Andrew Wommack

29. Ibid

30. *Conquering The Religious Spirit* by Tommi Femrite with Rebecca Wagner Sytsema copyright 2008 ISBN: 9780974548319 Gatekeepers International 15245 Jessie Drive, Colorado Springs, CO 80921 www.gatekeeppersintl.org

31. https://www.rcm-usa.org Foundational Renunciations Webinar by Diane Hawkins President of Restoration in Christ Ministries

32. Ibid

33. https://www.dailyom.com/journal/what-is-a-kundalini-awakening-and-how-can-one-change-your-life-

34. https://www.britannica.com/topic/New-Age-movement

35. https://www.aetherius.org/aura-chakras-kundalini/

36. https://www.hinduwebsite.com/hinduism/concepts/yoga.asp

37. https://www.rcm-usa.org Foundational Renunciations Webinar by Diane Hawkins President of Restoration in Christ Ministries

38. Ibid

39. *The Prophet's Dictionary the Ultimate Guide to Supernatural Wisdom*, copyright 1999, 2002, 2006

by Paula A. Price, Whitaker House 1030 Hunt Valley Circle, New Kensington, PA 15068

40. Ibid

41. https://en.wikipedia.org/wiki/Divination

42. *Webster's American 1828 Dictionary of the English Language* copyright 2010 by The Editorium LLC, West Valley City, UT 84128-3917, Walking Lion Press

43. Ibid

44. https://www.minotdailynews.com/news/local-news/2021/12/reflections-beware-of-the-leaven-of-the-pharisees-and-of-herod

45. *The Political Spirit* copyright 2008 by Faiscal Malick ISBN 10: 0-7684-27339 ISBN 13: 978-0-7684-2733-2; Destiny Image Publishers, Inc. P.O Box 310, Shippensburg, PA 17257-0310

46. Ibid

47. Ibid

48. *Webster's American 1828 Dictionary of the English Language* copyright 2010 by The Editorium LLC, West Valley City, UT 84128-3917, Walking Lion Press

49. *The Prophet's Dictionary the Ultimate Guide to Supernatural Wisdom*, copyright 1999, 2002, 2006 by Paula A. Price, Whitaker House 1030 Hunt Valley Circle, New Kensington, PA 15068

50. www.marthalucia.com Martha Lucia Prophet Watchman Christian International Ministries, Santa Rosa Beach, Florida

Bibliography

Books

Webster's American 1828 Dictionary of the English Language copyright 2010 by The Editorium LLC, West Valley City, UT 84128-3917, Walking Lion Press

Freemasonry Death in the Family copyright 2009 by Yvonne Kitchen ISBN: 0-646-34807-8 Fruitful Vine Publishing House 500 Kelletts Road Lysterfield Victoria 3156 Australia

Power and Prayers to Neutralize Leviathan copyright 2010 (The I found It! Series) by Joshua Tayo Obi-Gbesan ISBN: 9781609576493 www.zulonpress.com

A to Z Dream Symbology Dictionary by Dr. Barbie L Breathitt, DreamsDecoder.com, Copyright 2015 ISBN-13: 978-1-942551-02-7 Barbie Breathitt Enterprises, Inc.

Conquering The Religious Spirit by Tommi Femrite with Rebecca Wagner Sytsema copyright 2008 ISBN: 9780974548319 GateKeepers International 15245 Jessie

As in the Days of Midian

Drive, Colorado Springs, CO 80921

www.gatekeeppersintl.org

The Political Spirit copyright 2008 by Faiscal Malick ISBN 10: 0-7684-27339 ISBN 13: 978-0-7684-2733-2; Destiny Image Publishers, Inc. P.O Box 310, Shippensburg, PA 17257-0310

The Prophet's Dictionary the Ultimate Guide to Supernatural Wisdom, copyright 1999, 2002, 2006 by Paula A. Price, Whitaker House 1030 Hunt Valley Circle, New Kensington, PA 15068

DVD

Freemasonry; Unlocking Their Secrets DVD and MP4 https://www.ramministry.org/ Sylvie Sudduth

Websites

https://www.visionchurchci.org/ Word of the Lord 2023 by Prophet Bill Lackie, Christian International Ministries, Santa Rosa Beach, Florida 32459

https://aslansplace.com/language/en/author/paulcox15588/, Aslan's Place, Paul L. Cox

https://www.visionchurchci.org/ Bishop Bill Hamon, Christian International Ministries, Santa Rosa Beach, Florida 32459

https://www.aconsciousrethink.com/13929/signs-playing-mind-games/

https://www.greatbiblestudy.com/deliverance-ministry/religious-spirits/

https://www.charisbiblecollege.com Heart Essence of the Gospel, Charis Bible College by Andrew Wommack

https://www.rcm-usa.org Foundational Renunciations Webinar by Diane Hawkins President of Restoration in Christ Ministries

https://en.wikipedia.org/wiki/Divination

As in the Days of Midian

https://www.minotdailynews.com/news/local-news/2021/12/reflections-beware-of-the-leaven-of-the-pharisees-and-of-herod

https://www.marthalucia.com Martha Lucia Prophet Watchman Christian International Ministries, Santa Rosa Beach, Florida 32459

https://www.dailyom.com/journal/what-is-a-kundalini-awakening-and-how-can-one-change-your-life-

https://www.britannica.com/topic/New-Age-movement

https://www.aetherius.org/aura-chakras-kundalini/

https://www.hinduwebsite.com/hinduism/concepts/yoga.asp

More from the Author

A Baptism of Fiery Love is Coming

The Holy Spirit is at work in every person's life wooing and pursuing them to return to a loving relationship with Father God their Creator. This an individual process walked out by each person.

The Holy Spirit wants to introduce himself to each one of us. He came to heal our hearts and our bodies that we may have an abundant life and share in His glory. This is the beginning of an era of seeing and experiencing God's glory.

What Kind of Love is This?

With a burden to pray for the sick, Susan witnessed legs grow out, addictions leave, hips calcify causing patients to come off of long-term bed rest, and a dementia patient begin to have a clear mind. She learned the love of God through one miraculous encounter after another, including angels and divine intervention. Be empowered in the supernatural and receive an impartation for the miraculous love of God!

185

Revealing God's Truth on Abortion

A Study Guide to *God, What is My Baby's Name?*

"Whether you're a woman who has suffered in silence, a family member or friend with a loved one who has had an abortion, or a pastor or counselor, this book will provide insight, strategy and a practical process to restore hope and wholeness to broken lives."

—Jane Hamon

Five Smooth Stones to Slay Intimidation

God does not send us into battle without weapons. He has given us five smooth stones just like He gave to David to use against Goliath, the voice of intimidation that wants to rise up in our lives. We do not ever have to be intimidated or shut down again. Know your identity and authority God has given you. Walk in the love and grace from God that causes us to overcome all obstacles. Secure your smooth stone of humility that says, "I trust you Lord." With these five smooth stones in your sling of faith, you will slay the voice of intimidation in your life.

Stop Steven, Stop

. . . the angel yelled chasing after him

God does intervene in our lives and helps us and protects us from harm. He wants to be a Father to us and impart His love into us. The trauma of a child prematurely losing their life to alcohol, or a chemical overdose is felt by many families. This can cause grief to weigh upon our hearts. It is through the Holy Spirit's comfort and being in a loving relational environment that heals the pain of a broken heart!

Restoring Your Heart

Susan Pender shares revelation that she received from God in a dream indicating wounds that needed to mend to restore her heart and soul. She relates her personal experience to the story of Nehemiah who was moved with compassion to assist the people to repair and rebuild the city walls and gates of Jerusalem. Susan shares how the Holy Spirit moved with compassion in her life to bring restoration to the shattered fragments of her heart and soul.

When someone is wounded by physical, mental, emotional, or sexual traumatic events, part of their heart and soul can separate from their whole personhood. These separated parts will hold the painful emotions associated with the traumatic memory. The more someone's heart and soul are harmed in this way, the more they become literally broken within.

We may not even be aware of the painful memory that caused the trauma, but the Holy Spirit knows everything about us and can help us bring restoration to our hearts and souls and wholeness to our lives. God sent His Son Jesus to earth to die for us and the Holy Spirit to help and comfort us to restore our hearts.

God uses the metaphor of a city to describe us.

The LORD is building up Jerusalem; He is gathering [together] the exiles of Israel. He heals the brokenhearted, And binds up their wounds [healing their pain and comforting their sorrow]."

Psalm 147:2, 3, AMP

The ruins and desolate places reveal areas that are broken within you. The exiles are all the broken pieces of your heart and soul that need to be healed and integrated back into their rightful places within you to make you whole again. God wants to restore the walls and gates of your life to make you strong in Him again.

For Speaking Engagements or Questions
Contact Susan Marie Pender
Susanmariepender@gmail.com
www.lilyofthevalleyhealing.com